Coaching Youth Basketball

FOURTH EDITION

American Sport Education Program

HUMAN KINETICS

Library of Congress Cataloging-in-Publication Data

Coaching youth basketball / American Sport Education Program.-- 4th ed.
   p. cm.
   ISBN 0-7360-6450-8 (soft cover)
   1. Basketball for children--Coaching. 2. Basketball--Coaching. I. American Sport Education Program.
   GV885.3.C63 2007
   796.32307'7--dc22

                                        2006007410

ISBN-10: 0-7360-6450-8
ISBN-13: 978-0-7360-6450-7

The Web addresses cited in this text were current as of May 2006, unless otherwise noted.

Acquisitions Editor: Amy Tocco; **Project Writer:** Don Showalter; **Developmental Editor:** Laura Floch; **Assistant Editor:** Cory Weber; **Copyeditor:** Pat Connolly; **Proofreader:** Ann M. Augspurger; **Permission Manager:** Carly Breeding; **Graphic Designer:** Nancy Rasmus; **Graphic Artist:** Sandra Meier; **Photo Manager:** Dan Wendt; **Cover Designer:** Keith Blomberg; **Photographer (cover):** © Tim Porco/Sweet Spot Photos; **Photographer (interior):** Sarah Ritz, unless otherwise noted; **Art Manager:** Kareema McLendon; **Illustrator:** Kareema McLendon; **Printer:** United Graphics

We thank Mid-Prairie High School in Wellman, Iowa, for assistance in providing the location for the photo shoot for this book.

Copies of this book are available at special discounts for bulk purchase for sales promotions, premiums, fund-raising, or educational use. Special editions or book excerpts can also be created to specifications. For details, contact the Special Sales Manager at Human Kinetics.

Printed in the United States of America   10 9 8 7 6 5 4 3 2 1

Human Kinetics
Web site: www.HumanKinetics.com

United States: Human Kinetics
P.O. Box 5076
Champaign, IL 61825-5076
800-747-4457
e-mail: humank@hkusa.com

Canada: Human Kinetics
475 Devonshire Road Unit 100
Windsor, ON N8Y 2L5
800-465-7301 (in Canada only)
e-mail: orders@hkcanada.com

Europe: Human Kinetics
107 Bradford Road
Stanningley
Leeds LS28 6AT, United Kingdom
+44 (0) 113 255 5665
e-mail: hk@hkeurope.com

Australia: Human Kinetics
57A Price Avenue
Lower Mitcham, South Australia 5062
08 8277 1555
e-mail: liaw@hkaustralia.com

New Zealand: Human Kinetics
Division of Sports Distributors NZ Ltd.
P.O. Box 300 226 Albany
North Shore City
Auckland
0064 9 448 1207
e-mail: info@humankinetics.co.nz

Contents

Welcome to Coaching

Coaching young people is an exciting way to be involved in sport. But it isn't easy. Some coaches are overwhelmed by the responsibilities involved in helping players through their early sport experiences. And that's not surprising because coaching youngsters requires more than simply bringing the balls to the court and letting the players play. It also involves preparing those players physically and mentally to compete effectively, fairly, and safely in their sport, as well as providing them with a positive role model.

This book will help you meet the challenges and experience the many rewards of coaching young players. You'll learn how to meet your responsibilities as a coach, how to communicate well and provide for safety, and how to teach technical and tactical skills while keeping them fun. You'll also learn strategies for coaching on game day. To help you with your practices, over 30 drills are included throughout the text and in one of the book's appendixes. We also provide sample practice plans and season plans to help guide you throughout your season.

This book serves as a text for ASEP's Coaching Youth Basketball course. If you would like more information about this course or other American Sport Education Program courses and resources, please contact us at the following address:

ASEP
P.O. Box 5076
Champaign, IL 61825-5076
800-747-5698
www.ASEP.com

Drill Finder

Key to Diagrams

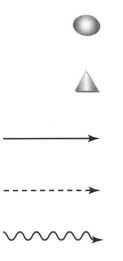

Offensive player

Defensive player

Player movement

Pass

Dribble

Stepping Into Coaching

I f you are like most youth league coaches, you have probably been recruited from the ranks of concerned parents, sport enthusiasts, or community volunteers. Like many rookie and veteran coaches, you probably have had little formal instruction on how to coach. But when the call went out for coaches to assist with the local youth basketball program, you answered because you like children and enjoy basketball, and perhaps because you wanted to be involved in a worthwhile community activity.

Your initial coaching assignment may be difficult. Like many volunteers, you may not know everything there is to know about basketball or about how to work with children. *Coaching Youth Basketball* presents the basics of coaching basketball effectively. To start, we look at your responsibilities and what's involved in being a coach. We also talk about what to do when your own child is on the team you coach, and we examine five tools for being an effective coach.

Your Responsibilities As a Coach

Coaching at all levels involves much more than designing offensive plays or drawing up defenses. Coaching involves accepting the tremendous responsibility you face when parents put their children into your care. As a basketball coach, you'll be called on to do the following:

1. *Provide a safe physical environment.*

   Playing basketball holds inherent risks, but as a coach you're responsible for regularly inspecting the courts and equipment used for practice and competition (see "Facilities and Equipment Checklist" in appendix A on page 136).

2. *Communicate in a positive way.*

   As you can already see, you have a lot to communicate. You'll communicate not only with your players and their parents but also with the coaching staff, officials, administrators, and others. Communicate in a way that is positive and that demonstrates that you have the best interests of the players at heart (see chapter 2 for more information).

3. *Teach the fundamental skills of basketball.*

   When teaching the fundamental skills of basketball, keep in mind that basketball is a game, and therefore, you want to be sure that your players have fun. We ask that you help all players be the best they can be by creating a fun, yet productive, practice environment. To help you do this, we'll show you an innovative "games approach" to teaching and practicing the skills young players need to know—an approach that kids thoroughly enjoy (see chapter 5 for more information). Additionally, to help your players improve their skills, you need to have a sound understanding of offensive and defensive skills. We'll provide information to assist you in gaining that understanding (see chapters 7 and 8).

4. *Teach the rules of basketball.*

Coaching Tip
Set a goal for yourself to make at least two positive comments to each player during each practice.

You need to introduce the rules of basketball and incorporate them into individual instruction (see chapter 3 for more information). Many rules can be taught in practice, including offensive rules (such as double dribble, traveling, the three-second rule, over-and-back violations, and free throw violations) as well as defensive rules (such as fouling and the five-second rule on closely guarding an opponent). You should also plan to review the rules and go over them with your players any time an opportunity naturally arises in practices.

5. *Direct players in competition.*

Your responsibilities include determining starting lineups and a substitution plan, relating appropriately to officials and to opposing coaches and players, and making sound tactical decisions during games (see chapter 9 for more information on coaching during games). Remember that the focus is not on winning at all costs, but on coaching your kids to compete well, do their best, improve their basketball skills, and strive to win within the rules.

6. *Help your players become fit and value fitness for a lifetime.*

We want you to help your players be fit so they can play basketball safely and successfully. We also want your players to learn to become fit on their own, understand the value of fitness, and enjoy training. Thus, we ask you not to make them do push-ups or run laps for punishment. Make it fun to get fit for basketball, and make it fun to play basketball so that they'll stay fit for a lifetime.

7. *Help young people develop character.*

Character development includes learning, caring, being honest and respectful, and taking responsibility. These intangible qualities are no less important to teach to your players than the skill of shooting the basketball. We ask you to teach these values to players by demonstrating and encouraging behaviors that express these values at all times. For example, in teaching good team defense, stress to young players the importance of learning their assignments, helping their teammates, playing within the rules, showing respect for their opponents, and understanding that they are responsible for winning the individual battle on every play—even though they may not be recognized individually for their efforts.

These are your responsibilities as a coach. Remember that every player is an individual. You must provide a wholesome environment in which every player has the opportunity to learn how to play the game without fear while having fun and enjoying the overall basketball experience.

Coaching Your Own Child

Coaching can become even more complicated when your child plays on the team you coach. Many coaches are parents, but the two roles should not be confused. As a parent, you are responsible for yourself and your child, but as a coach you are also responsible for the organization, all the players on the team, and their parents. Because of this additional responsibility, your behavior on the basketball floor will be different from your behavior at home, and your son or daughter may not understand why.

> **Coaching Tip**
> When coaching your own child, a good rule to follow is to not bring up the topic of basketball at home unless your child initiates the conversation.

For example, imagine the confusion of a young boy who is the center of his parents' attention at home but is barely noticed by his father (who is the coach) in the sport setting. Or consider the mixed signals received by a young girl whose skill is constantly evaluated by a coach (who is also her mother) who otherwise rarely comments on her daughter's activities. You need to explain to your child your new responsibilities and how they will affect your relationship when coaching. Take the following steps to avoid problems in coaching your own child:

- Ask your child if he or she wants you to coach the team.
- Explain why you want to be involved with the team.
- Discuss with your child how your interactions will change when you take on the role of coach at practices or games.
- Limit your coaching behavior to when you are in the coaching role.
- Avoid parenting during practice or game situations to keep your role clear in your child's mind.
- Reaffirm your love for your child, irrespective of his or her performance on the basketball court.

Five Tools of an Effective Coach

Have you purchased the traditional coaching tools—things such as whistles, coaching clothes, sport shoes, and a clipboard? They'll help you in the act of coaching, but to be successful, you'll need five other tools that cannot be bought. These tools are available only through self-examination and hard work; they're easy to remember with the acronym COACH:

C	Comprehension
O	Outlook
A	Affection
C	Character
H	Humor

Comprehension

Comprehension of the rules and skills of basketball is required. You must understand the elements of the sport. To improve your comprehension of basketball, take the following steps:

- Read about the rules of basketball in chapter 3 of this book.
- Read about the fundamental skills of basketball in chapters 7 and 8.
- Read additional basketball coaching books, including those available from the American Sport Education Program (ASEP).
- Contact youth basketball organizations.
- Attend basketball coaching clinics.
- Talk with more experienced coaches.
- Observe local college, high school, and youth basketball games.
- Watch basketball games on television.

In addition to having basketball knowledge, you must implement proper training and safety methods so that your players can participate with little risk of injury. Even then, injuries may occur. And more often than not, you'll be the first person responding to your players' injuries, so be sure you understand the basic emergency care procedures described in chapter 4. Also, read in that chapter how to handle more serious sport injury situations.

Outlook

This coaching tool refers to your perspective and goals—what you seek as a coach. The most common coaching objectives are to (a) have fun; (b) help players develop their physical, mental, and social skills; and (c) strive to win. Thus, your outlook involves your priorities, your planning, and your vision for the future. See "Assessing Your Priorities" (page 6) to learn more about the priorities you set for yourself as a coach.

Assessing Your Priorities

Even though all coaches focus on competition, we want you to focus on *positive* competition—keeping the pursuit of victory in perspective by making decisions that, first, are in the best interest of the players, and second, will help to win the game.

So, how do you know if your outlook and priorities are in order? Here's a little test:

1. Which situation would you be most proud of?
   a. knowing that each participant enjoyed playing basketball
   b. seeing that all players improved their basketball skills
   c. winning the league championship

2. Which statement best reflects your thoughts about sport?
   a. If it isn't fun, don't do it.
   b. Everyone should learn something every day.
   c. Sport isn't fun if you don't win.

3. How would you like your players to remember you?
   a. as a coach who was fun to play for
   b. as a coach who provided a good base of fundamental skills
   c. as a coach who had a winning record

4. Which would you most like to hear a parent of a player on your team say?
   a. Mike really had a good time playing basketball this year.
   b. Nicole learned some important lessons playing basketball this year.
   c. Willie played on the first-place basketball team this year.

5. Which of the following would be the most rewarding moment of your season?
   a. having your team want to continue playing, even after practice is over
   b. seeing one of your players finally master the skill of dribbling
   c. winning the league championship

Look over your answers. If you most often selected "a" responses, then having fun is most important to you. A majority of "b" answers suggests that skill development is what attracts you to coaching. And if "c" was your most frequent response, winning is tops on your list of coaching priorities. If your priorities are in order, your players' well-being will take precedence over your team's win–loss record every time.

ASEP has a motto that will help you keep your outlook in line with the best interests of the kids on your team. It summarizes in four words all you need to remember when establishing your coaching priorities:

Athletes First, Winning Second

This motto recognizes that striving to win is an important, even vital, part of sports. But it emphatically states that no efforts in striving to win should be made at the expense of the players' well-being, development, and enjoyment. Take the following actions to better define your outlook:

- With the members of your coaching staff, determine your priorities for the season.
- Prepare for situations that may challenge your priorities.
- Set goals for yourself and your players that are consistent with your priorities.
- Plan how you and your players can best attain your goals.
- Review your goals frequently to be sure that you are staying on track.

Affection

Another vital tool you will want to have in your coaching kit is a genuine concern for the young people you coach. This requires having a passion for kids, a desire to share with them your enjoyment and knowledge of basketball, and the patience and understanding that allow all your players to grow from their involvement in sport. You can demonstrate your affection and patience in many ways, including the following:

- Make an effort to get to know each player on your team.
- Treat each player as an individual.
- Empathize with players trying to learn new and difficult skills.
- Treat players as you would like to be treated under similar circumstances.
- Control your emotions.
- Show your enthusiasm for being involved with your team.
- Keep an upbeat tempo and positive tone in all of your communications.

Character

The fact that you have decided to coach young basketball players probably means that you think participation in sport is important. But whether that participation develops character in your players depends as much on you as it does on the sport itself. How can you help your players build character?

Having good character means modeling appropriate behaviors for sport and life. That means more than just saying the right things. What you say and what you do must match. There is no place in coaching for the "Do as I say, not as I do" philosophy. Challenge, support, encourage, and reward every youngster, and your players will be more likely to accept, even celebrate, their differences. Be in control before, during, and after all practices and games. And don't be afraid to admit that you were wrong. No one is perfect!

Each member of your coaching staff should consider the following steps to becoming a good role model:

- Take stock of your strengths and weaknesses.
- Build on your strengths.
- Set goals for yourself to improve on areas that are not as strong.
- If you slip up, apologize to your team and to yourself. You'll do better next time.

Humor

Humor is an often-overlooked coaching tool. It means having the ability to laugh at yourself and with your players during practices and games. Nothing helps balance the seriousness of a skill session like a chuckle or two. And a sense of humor puts in perspective the many mistakes your players will make. So don't get upset over each miscue or respond negatively to erring players. Allow your players and yourself to enjoy the ups, and don't dwell on the downs. Here are some tips for injecting humor and fun into your practices:

- Make practices fun by including a variety of activities.
- Keep all players involved in games and skill practices.
- Consider laughter by your players to be a sign of enjoyment, not of waning discipline.
- Smile!

Communicating As a Coach

In chapter 1, you learned about the tools you need for coaching: comprehension, outlook, affection, character, and humor. These are essentials for effective coaching; without them, you'd have a difficult time getting started. But none of the tools will work if you don't know how to use them with your players—and this requires skillful communication. This chapter examines what communication is and how you can become a more effective communicator.

Coaches often mistakenly believe that communication occurs only when instructing players to do something, but verbal commands are only a small part of the communication process. More than half of what is communicated is done so nonverbally. So remember when you are coaching: Actions speak louder than words.

Communication in its simplest form involves two people: a sender and a receiver. The sender transmits the message verbally, through facial expressions, and possibly through body language. Once the message is sent, the receiver must receive it and, optimally, understand it. A receiver who fails to pay attention or listen will miss part, if not all, of the message.

Sending Effective Messages

Young players often have little understanding of the rules and skills of basketball and probably even less confidence in their ability to play the game. So they need accurate, understandable, and supportive messages to help them along. That's why your verbal and nonverbal messages are important.

Verbal Messages

"Sticks and stones may break my bones, but words will never hurt me" isn't true. Spoken words can have a strong and long-lasting effect. And coaches' words are particularly influential because youngsters place great importance on what coaches say. Like many former youth sport participants, you may have a difficult time remembering much of anything you were told by your elementary school teachers, but you can probably still recall several specific things your coaches at that level said to you. Such is the lasting effect of a coach's comments to a player.

Whether you are correcting misbehavior, teaching a player how to pass the ball, or praising a player for good effort, you should consider a number of things when sending a message verbally:

- Be positive and honest.
- State it clearly and simply.
- Say it loud enough, and say it again.
- Be consistent.

Be Positive and Honest

Nothing turns people off like hearing someone nag all the time, and players react similarly to a coach who gripes constantly. Kids particularly need encouragement because they often doubt their ability to perform in a sport. So look for and tell your players what they did well.

But don't cover up poor or incorrect play with rosy words of praise. Kids know all too well when they've erred, and no cheerfully expressed cliché can undo their mistakes. If you fail to acknowledge players' errors, your players will think you are a phony.

An effective way to correct a performance error is to first point out the part of the skill that the player performed correctly. Then explain—in a positive manner—the error that the player made and show him the correct way to do it. Finish by encouraging the player and emphasizing the correct performance.

Be sure not to follow a positive statement with the word *but*. For example, you shouldn't say, "That was a good decision to pass, Kelly, but if you'd follow through with your fingers pointing toward your target you'd get better accuracy." This causes many kids to ignore the positive statement and focus on the negative one. Instead, you should say something like, "That was a good decision to pass, Kelly—way to spot those openings! Next time, try following through with your fingers pointing toward the target, and I bet you'll notice your pass gets more accuracy. Great job moving the ball out there!"

State It Clearly and Simply

Positive and honest messages are good, but only if expressed directly in words your players understand. Beating around the bush is ineffective and inefficient. And if you ramble, your players will miss the point of your message and probably lose interest. Here are some tips for saying things clearly:

- Organize your thoughts before speaking to your players.
- Know your subject as completely as possible.
- Explain things thoroughly, but don't bore your players with long-winded monologues.
- Use language your players can understand, and be consistent in your terminology. However, avoid trying to be hip by using their age group's slang.

Say It Loud Enough, and Say It Again

Talk to your team in a voice that all members can hear. A crisp, vigorous voice commands attention and respect; garbled and weak speech is tuned out. It's okay and, in fact, appropriate to soften your voice when speaking to a player individually about a personal problem. But most of the time your messages will be for all your players to hear, so make sure they can! An enthusiastic voice also motivates players and tells them you enjoy being their coach. A word of caution, however: Avoid dominating the setting with a booming voice that distracts attention from players' performances.

Coaching Tip
Remember, terms that you are familiar with and understand may be completely foreign to your players, especially younger players or beginners. You may need to use demonstrations with the players so they can "see" the term and how it relates to the game of basketball.

Sometimes what you say, even if stated loudly and clearly, won't sink in the first time. This may be particularly true when young players hear words they don't understand. To avoid boring repetition and still get your message across, you can say the same thing in a slightly different way. For instance, you might first tell your players, "Guard your opponents tighter!" If they don't appear to understand, you might say, "When your opponents are in scoring range, be sure to be close enough to them to make the shot or the pass difficult." The second form of the message may get through to players who missed it the first time around.

Be Consistent

People often say things in ways that imply a different message. For example, a touch of sarcasm added to the words "Way to go!" sends an entirely different message than the words themselves suggest. You should avoid sending mixed messages. Keep the tone of your voice consistent with the words you use. And don't say something one day and contradict it the next; players will get their wires crossed.

You also want to keep your terminology consistent. Many basketball terms describe the same or similar skills. One coach may use the term *hedge on the screens* to describe how to defend a pick-and-roll, while another coach may call this *showing your numbers* on the screen. Although both are correct, to be consistent as a staff, the coaches of a team should agree on all terms before the start of the season and then stay with them.

Nonverbal Messages

Just as you should be consistent in the tone of voice and words you use, you should also keep your verbal and nonverbal messages consistent. An extreme example of failing to do this would be shaking your head, indicating disapproval, while at the same time telling a player "Nice try." Which is the player to believe, your gesture or your words?

Messages can be sent nonverbally in several ways. Facial expressions and body language are just two of the more obvious forms of nonverbal signals that can help you when you coach. Keep in mind that as a coach you need to be a teacher first, and any action that detracts from the message you are trying to convey should be avoided.

Facial Expressions

The look on a person's face is the quickest clue to what the person thinks or feels. Your players know this, so they will study your face, looking for a sign that will tell them more than the words you say. Don't try to fool them by putting on a happy or blank "mask." They'll see through it, and you'll lose credibility.

Serious, stone-faced expressions provide no cues to kids who want to know how they are performing. When faced with this, kids will just assume you're unhappy or disinterested. Don't be afraid to smile. A smile from a coach can give a great boost to an unsure player. Plus, a smile lets your players know that you are happy coaching them. But don't overdo it, or your players won't be able to tell when you are genuinely pleased by something they've done or when you are just putting on a smiling face.

Body Language

What would your players think you were feeling if you came to practice slouched over, with your head down and your shoulders slumped? Would they think you were tired, bored, or unhappy? What would they think you were feeling if you watched them during a game with your hands on your hips, your jaws clenched, and your face reddened? Would they think you were upset with them, disgusted at an official, or mad at a fan? Probably some or all of these things would enter your players' minds. And none is the impression you want your players to have of you. That's why you should carry yourself in a pleasant, confident, and vigorous manner.

> **Coaching Tip**
> As a coach, you need to be aware of your body language. You must ensure that the players are translating it correctly and that you are providing a good example for your players to model.

Physical contact can also be a very important use of body language. A handshake, a pat on the head, an arm around the shoulder, and even a big hug are effective ways to show approval, concern, affection, and joy to your players. Youngsters are especially in need of this type of nonverbal message. Keep within the obvious moral and legal limits, of course, but don't be reluctant to touch your players, sending a message that can only be expressed in that way.

Improving Receiving Skills

Now let's examine the other half of the communication process: receiving messages. Too often very good senders are very poor receivers of messages. But as a coach of young players, you must be able to fulfill both roles effectively.

The requirements for receiving messages are quite simple, but receiving skills are perhaps less satisfying and therefore underdeveloped compared to sending skills. People seem to enjoy hearing themselves talk more than they enjoy hearing others talk. But if you learn the keys to receiving messages and make a strong effort to use them with your players, you'll be surprised by what you've been missing.

Pay Attention

First, you must pay attention; you must want to hear what others have to communicate to you. That's not always easy when you're busy coaching and have many things competing for your attention. But in one-on-one or team meetings with players, you must focus on what they are telling you, both verbally and nonverbally. You'll be amazed at the little signals you pick up. Not only will this focused attention help you catch every word your players say, but you'll also notice your players' moods and physical states. In addition, you'll get an idea of your players' feelings toward you and other players on the team.

Listen Carefully

How you receive messages from others, perhaps more than anything else you do, demonstrates how much you care for the sender and what that person has to tell you. If you care little for your players or have little regard for what they have to say, it will show in how you attend and listen to them. You need to check yourself. Do you find your mind wandering to what you are going to do after practice while one of your players is talking to you? Do you frequently have to ask your players, "What did you say?" If so, you need to work on your receiving mechanics of attending and listening. But if you find that you're constantly missing the messages your players send, perhaps the most critical question you should ask yourself is this: Do I want to be a coach?

Providing Feedback

So far we've discussed separately the sending and receiving of messages. But we all know that senders and receivers switch roles several times during an interaction. One person initiates a communication by sending a message to another person, who then receives the message. The receiver then becomes the sender by responding to the person who sent the initial message. These verbal and nonverbal responses are called *feedback*.

Your players will look to you for feedback all the time. They will want to know how you think they are performing, what you think of their ideas, and whether their efforts please you. You can respond in many different ways, and how you respond will strongly affect your players. They will react most favorably to positive feedback.

Praising players when they have performed or behaved well is an effective way of getting them to repeat (or try to repeat) that behavior. And positive feedback for effort is an especially effective way to motivate youngsters to work on difficult skills. So rather than shouting at and providing negative feedback to players who have made mistakes, you should try offering positive feedback and letting them know what they did correctly and how they can improve. Sometimes just the way you word feedback can make it more positive than negative. For example, instead of saying, "Don't shoot the ball that way," you might say, "Shoot the ball this way." Then your players will be focusing on what to do instead of what not to do.

Positive feedback can be verbal or nonverbal. Telling young players, especially in front of teammates, that they have performed well is a great way to boost their confidence. And a pat on the back or a handshake communicates that you recognize a player's performance.

Communicating With Other Groups

In addition to sending and receiving messages and providing feedback to players, coaching also involves interacting with members of the coaching staff, parents, fans, officials, and opposing coaches. If you don't communicate effectively with these groups, your coaching career will be unpleasant and short lived. So try the following suggestions for communicating with these groups.

Coaching Staff

Before you hold your first practice, the coaching staff should meet and discuss the roles and responsibilities that each coach will undertake during the year. Depending on the number of assistant coaches, the staff responsibilities can be divided into different areas. For example, one coach may be in charge of the defenses played, while another is responsible for the offensive sets. The head coach has the final responsibility for all phases of the game, but as much as possible, the assistant coaches should be responsible for their areas.

Before practices start, the coaching staff must also discuss and agree on terminology, plans for practice, schemes, game day organization, the method of communicating during practice and games, and game conditions. The coaches on your staff must present a united front and speak with one voice, and they must all take a similar approach to coaching, interaction with the players and parents, and interaction with one another. Disagreements should be discussed away from the court, and each coach should have a say as the staff comes to an agreement.

Coaching Tip
Your coaching staff must be organized before practices and games. Work with your staff to ensure that tasks are completed. Each staff member should be responsible for a specific task in an effort to use time more efficiently. This will enable you to focus on the actual practice or game.

Parents

A player's parents need to be assured that their son or daughter is under the direction of a coach who is both knowledgeable about the sport and concerned about the youngster's well-being. You can put their worries to rest by holding a preseason parent-orientation meeting in which you describe your background and your approach to coaching (see "Preseason Meeting Topics").

Preseason Meeting Topics

1. Outline the paperwork that is needed:
   - Copy of the player's birth certificate
   - Completed player's application and payment record
   - Report card from the previous year
   - Participation agreement form
   - Informed consent form

2. Go over the inherent risks of basketball and other safety issues.

3. Inform parents of the date and time that uniforms and equipment will be handed out.

4. Review the season practice schedule, including the date, location, and time of each practice.

5. Go over the proper gear and attire that should be worn at each practice session.

6. Discuss nutrition, hydration, and rest for players.

7. Explain the goals for the team.

8. Cover methods of communication: e-mail list, emergency phone numbers, interactive Web site, and so on.

9. Discuss ways that parents can help with the team.

10. Discuss standards of conduct for coaches, players, and parents.

11. Provide time for questions and answers.

If parents contact you with comments or concerns during the season, you should listen to them closely and try to offer positive responses or solutions. If you need to communicate with parents, it is best to catch them after a practice, give them a phone call, or send a note through e-mail or the U.S. mail. Messages sent to parents through young players are too often lost, misinterpreted, or forgotten.

Fans

The stands probably won't be overflowing at your games, which means that you'll more easily hear the few fans who criticize your coaching. When you hear something negative about the job you're doing, don't respond. Keep calm, consider whether the message had any value, and if not, forget it. Acknowledging critical, unwarranted comments from a fan during a game will only encourage others to voice their opinions. So put away your "rabbit ears" and communicate to fans, through your actions, that you are a confident, competent coach.

You must also prepare your players for fans' criticisms. Tell your players that it is you, not the spectators, that they should listen to. If you notice that one of your players is rattled by a fan's comment, you should reassure the player that your evaluation is more objective and favorable—and the one that counts.

Officials

How you communicate with officials will have a great influence on the way your players behave toward them. Therefore, you must set a good example. Greet officials with a handshake, an introduction, and perhaps casual conversation about the upcoming game. Indicate your respect for them before, during, and after the game. Don't shout, make nasty remarks, or use disrespectful body gestures. Your players will see you do it, and they'll get the idea that such behavior is appropriate. Plus, if the official hears or sees you, the communication between the two of you will break down.

Opposing Coaches

Make an effort to visit with the coach of the opposing team before the game. During the game, don't get into a personal feud with the opposing coach. Remember, it's the kids, not the coaches, who are competing. And by getting along well with the opposing coach, you'll show your players that competition involves cooperation.

Understanding Rules and Equipment

B asketball is a complicated game played by two teams in a relatively small space, with the players designated by positions. The game is governed by a thick rule book. This introduction to the basic rules of basketball won't cover every rule of the game but instead will give you what you need to work with players who are 6 to 14 years old. In this chapter, we cover specifics about some of the basics of the game, such as the number of players, ball and court size, and game length, depending on your team's age group. We also describe specifics such as equipment, player positions, scoring, fouls, and how to start and restart games. We wrap things up by describing officiating and identifying some of the most common officiating signals.

Age Modifications for Basketball

Before we begin, let's consider some of the modifications that can be made to accommodate different age groups. Things such as the size of the court, the size of the ball, the number of players on the court, and the duration of the game can be adjusted for the various age groups to help accommodate players' development and skill levels. Suggested adjustments are as follows:

	6 to 8 years	9 to 11 years	12 to 14 years
Players on team	5	5	5
Players on court	5v5	5v5	5v5
Ball size	Junior (#5)	Women's (#6)	Regulation (#7, or #6 in some states)
Court size	Short court	Short court	Full court
Free throw distance	9 ft.	9 ft.	12-15 ft.
Game length	24 min.	24 min.	32 min.
Time-outs	4	4	4
Basket height	7 ft.	8 ft.	9-10 ft.

How the Game Is Played

Basketball is a fast-paced game where the objective is to put the ball into the basket. Although the concept is simple, specific offensive and defensive aspects of the game are executed differently based on the level of play and the game situation. Additionally, the court that the game is played on may vary depending on the age level of your players and the facility where the game is played. Figure 3.1 shows the court markings for a standard basketball court.

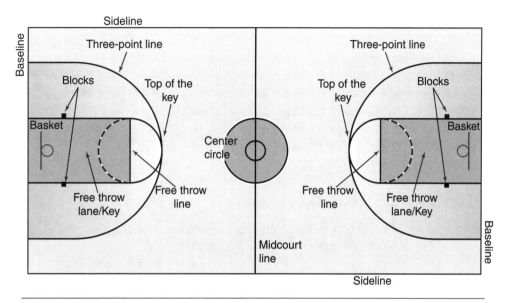

Figure 3.1   Basketball court area.

Several areas of the court shown in figure 3.1 are referred to with special basketball terminology. Here are a few definitions:

- *Frontcourt.* Refers to the half of the court where your team's offensive basket is located.
- *Backcourt.* Includes the midcourt line and the half of the court where your opponent's basket is located.
- *Blocks.* Square markings six feet from the baseline on each side of the lane.
- *Perimeter.* The area outside the three-second lane area.
- *Three-point line.* A semicircle that is 19 feet, 9 inches from the basket at all points. Shots that are made from behind this line count for three points instead of two.
- *Free throw lane/Key.* The area that extends from the baseline under the basket to the free throw line; it's also called the *three-second lane.*
- *Top of the key.* The semicircle that extends beyond the free throw line.

Player Equipment

Basketball requires very little player equipment. Players should wear basketball shoes so they have proper traction on the court. They should wear

Coaching Tip

You should ensure that each player on your team is outfitted properly and correctly. Early in the season, before games begin, take time out of practice to demonstrate how uniforms and equipment should be handled and worn.

clothing such as athletic shorts and tank tops or loose-fitting shirts so they have the freedom of movement needed to run, jump, and shoot. Players may choose to wear safety glasses or goggles to protect their eyes from injury. Also, players who have conditions affecting the knees or elbows may want to wear soft pads to protect them. Players may *not* wear jewelry during games.

You must examine the condition of each item you distribute to players. Also make sure that the pieces of equipment they furnish themselves meet acceptable standards.

Player Positions

Young players should be given a chance to play a variety of positions, on both offense and defense. By playing different positions, they'll have a better all-around playing experience and may stay more interested in the sport. Furthermore, they'll gain a better understanding of the many technical and tactical skills used in the game. This will also help them appreciate the efforts of their teammates who play positions they find difficult.

Coaching Tip

For younger players, especially the 6 to 8 age group, you may find that it is more acceptable to not label your players by positions as you want your players to experiment with all positions.

Player positions in basketball are typically given a number (1 through 5) for each player on the court. Following are descriptions of these positions.

- *Guards.* A basketball team usually has two guards in the game at all times. The guards play farthest from the basket, on the perimeter. The point guard (the 1 position) is played by the team's best dribbler and passer. The off-guard (the 2 position) is often played by the best long-range shooter and second-best dribbler. Guards are usually the best ball handlers and outside shooters on the team. They tend to be shorter and quicker than the other players and have good dribbling and passing skills.

- *Forwards.* A team usually plays with two forwards in its lineup. Forwards are typically taller than guards, and they play closer to the basket. The smaller forward (the 3 position) is also referred to as the *wing*, and this position is often filled by the most versatile and athletic member of the team. This forward must be able to play in the lane and on the perimeter on offense, and on defense, he must be able to guard small and quick or big and strong opponents. The other forward position (the 4 position) is filled by a bigger player; this forward should be able to shoot the ball accurately from within 12 feet of the basket and rebound the ball when shots are missed. This is a good spot to assign to one of your bigger players and better rebounders—one who can also shoot the ball from anywhere in the lane area.

- *Center.* Most basketball teams designate one player on the court as their center. The center (the 5 position, which is also called the *post position*) is frequently the tallest or biggest player on the team. That extra size is helpful in maneuvering for shots or rebounds around the basket. A tall center can also make it difficult for opposing teams to shoot near the basket. A center should have "soft" hands to catch the passes thrown into the lane area by guards and forwards.

Rules of Play

Basketball rules are designed to make the game run smoothly and safely and to prevent either team from gaining an unfair advantage. Throw out the rules and a basketball game can quickly turn chaotic. Following is an overview of some of the basic rules in basketball.

Starts and Restarts

In regulation play, a jump ball at center court is used to start games and over-time periods, which are played when teams are tied at the end of regulation time. During jump balls, the official tosses up the ball between two players, usually each team's center or best leaper. Each player attempts to tip the ball to a teammate (who must be outside of the center circle) to gain possession of the ball. Another jump ball situation is simultaneous possession of the ball by players from opposing teams. In this case, teams alternate possession; the team that did not win the first jump ball takes the ball out of bounds in the next jump ball situation.

Play stops during intermissions and time-outs, but also when the ball goes out of bounds and when an official calls a violation or a foul (as discussed later in this chapter). The clock restarts when the ball is touched following an inbounds pass or a missed free throw.

Scoring

In regulation play, teams are awarded two points for every shot made from inside the three-point line, and they are given three points for shots made from beyond the three-point stripe. A successful free throw is worth one point. (Players may not enter the lane until the free throw has hit the rim. If the free throw doesn't hit the rim, the ball is awarded to the opposing team out of bounds.) The team that scores the most points over the course of the game is the winner.

Fouls

Basketball is a contact sport, with players in close proximity and in constant motion. The rules of the game discourage rough play or tactics that allow a team to gain an advantage through brute force. Therefore, fouls are called when officials see illegal physical contact between two or more players based on these principles:

- The first player to establish position (to become stationary or set) on the court has priority rights to that position.
- A body part cannot be extended into the path of an opponent.
- The player who moves into the path of an opponent—especially an airborne opponent—when contact occurs is responsible for the contact.
- All players have the right to the space extending straight up from their feet on the floor. This is called the *principle of verticality*.

A team that fouls too much pays for it, because fouls carry with them increasingly severe penalties. A player who has five fouls must sit out for the remainder of the game. In regulation play, a team that has more than a specified number of fouls in a quarter or half gives the opposing team a bonus situation: The member of the team who was fouled is allowed to shoot free throws. If the foul is a nonshooting—or personal—foul, the player shoots one free throw and, if she makes it, shoots a second one (this is called *one-and-one*). Table 3.1 lists the most common personal fouls and their penalties.

Table 3.1 Personal Fouls and Penalties

Type of foul	Description of foul	Penalty
Blocking	Physically impeding the progress of another player who is still moving.	Foul
Charging	Running into or pushing a defender who is stationary.	Foul
Hand-checking	Using the hands to check the progress of an offensive player when that player is in front of the defender who is using the hands.	Foul
Holding	Restricting the movement of an opponent.	Foul
Illegal screen	A form of blocking in which the player setting the screen is still moving when the defender makes contact.	Don't call except for the 12 to 14 age group
Over-the-back	Infringing on the vertical plane of, and making contact with, a player who is in position and attempting to rebound.	Don't call except for the 12 to 14 age group
Pushing	Impeding the progress or otherwise moving a player by pushing or shoving.	Foul
Reaching in	Extending an arm and making contact with a ball handler in an attempt to steal the ball.	Foul
Tripping	Extending a leg or foot and causing an opponent to lose balance or fall.	Foul

If the foul is a shooting foul—in other words, a foul in which a defender makes contact with a player who is shooting the basketball—the player shoots two free throws.

Emphasize to your players the importance of keeping their hands off the shooter, establishing position, using the feet to maintain position (rather than reaching in with the hands), and not attempting to rebound over an opponent who has established position.

Other types of fouls exist, such as a *technical foul*; this is a foul that does not involve contact with the opponent while the ball is alive (e.g., use of profanity, delay of game, unsporting conduct). *Intentional* and *flagrant fouls* relate to extreme behaviors and should not (we hope) come up with your players. If they do, players who are guilty of unsporting conduct during a game are usually ejected, assessed a technical foul, and should be counseled by the coach. In such a case, the opposing team is awarded two free throws and possession of the ball.

Violations

Violations are mistakes made by the offensive team that will result in the ball being given to the defensive team. Turnovers—the loss of the ball to the defense—caused by violations will be one of your continuing frustrations as a basketball coach. Violations are categorized as either ballhandling or clock violations. Table 3.2 shows our recommendations for modifying the rules for these violations based on the age group of your team.

Substitutions

A substitution is when a player that is out of the game will take the place of a player that is on the playing floor. Players coming into the game must go to the scorer's table and give the scorekeeper their number and the number of the player they are replacing so that this information can be recorded. The substitute must then wait at the scorer's table until the referee motions for him to enter the game. Substitutions can be any number of players (ranging from 1 to 5 players at a time) and are allowed at any time during stopped clock situations.

Time-Outs

A time-out is when the play stops so each coach can visit with their team off the playing floor. A time-out may be called by a player or a coach by giving the proper signal to the official during any dead-ball situation or if your team has possession of the ball. A time-out is designated as a 30-second time-out or a 1-minute time-out by the coach of the team that called it. Each team is allowed five time-outs (three 1-minute time-outs and two 30-second time-outs) per game with an extra 1-minute time-out allowed per each overtime.

Table 3.2 Rule Modifications for Violations

Violation	Description	Age group		
		6 to 8 years	9 to 11 years	12 to 14 years
Ballhandling violations				
Double dribble	Resuming dribbling after having stopped (when no defender interrupts the player's possession of the ball) or dribbling with both hands at the same time.	Allow one violation per player possession; gradually tighten up this allowance.	Allow one violation per player possession; gradually tighten up this allowance.	Call.
Over-and-back	The return of the ball to the backcourt when last touched by an offensive player in the frontcourt.	Don't call.	Don't call.	Don't call.
Traveling	Taking more than one step without dribbling; also called *carrying the ball or palming the ball* when a player turns the ball a complete rotation in the hand between dribbles.	Give an extra step for starting and stopping; gradually tighten up this allowance.	Give an extra step for starting and stopping; gradually tighten up this allowance.	Call.
Clock violations				
Inbounds	On any inbounds play, the player throwing the ball in has 5 seconds to release the ball.	Don't call.	Give warnings early in the season; call after midseason.	Call.
Lane	An offensive player cannot be in the lane (in the key) for more than 3 seconds at a time.	Don't call.	Give warnings early in the season; call after midseason.	Call.
Backcourt	A team must advance the ball into its frontcourt within 10 seconds after gaining possession in the backcourt.	Don't call.	Give warnings early in the season; call after midseason.	Call.
Shot clock	The ball must leave an offensive player's hands before the shot clock expires. The ball must subsequently hit the rim on that shot or it will be a violation.	Don't use.	Don't use.	Don't use.

Officiating

Basketball rules are enforced by officials. In youth basketball, there are typically two officials overseeing the game. Officials have many responsibilities during a game, including effectively communicating their calls to other members of the staff (such as the scorers and timers) and to the players, coaches, and spectators. Figure 3.2, *a* through *r*, shows some common officiating signals.

If you have a concern about how a game is being officiated, you should address the officials respectfully. Do so immediately if at any time you feel that the officiating jeopardizes the safety of your players.

Figure 3.2 Some signals commonly used by referees are *(a)* starting clock, *(b)* stopping clock for jump ball, *(c)* beckoning a sub in on a dead ball, *(d)* stopping clock for foul, *(e)* scoring one point (two fingers for scoring two points and three fingers for scoring three points).

(continued)

Figure 3.2 *(continued)* Some signals commonly used by referees are *(f)* blocking, *(g)* bonus situation, *(h)* over-and-back or carrying the ball, *(i)* pushing, *(j)* illegal use of hands, *(k)* technical foul.

Figure 3.2 *(continued)* Some signals commonly used by referees are *(l)* three-second violation, *(m)* designating out-of-bounds spot, *(n)* traveling, *(o)* holding, *(p)* no score, *(q)* illegal dribble, and *(r)* hand check.

4

Providing for Players' Safety

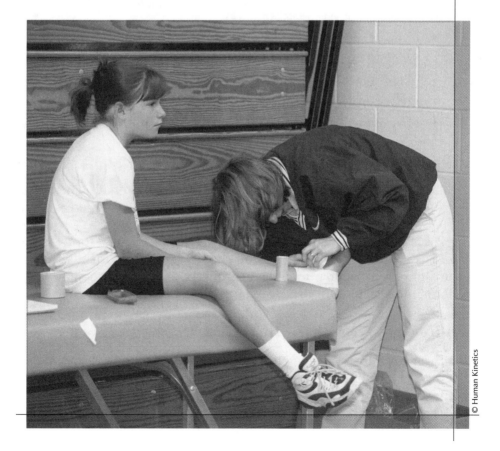

One of your players appears to break free downcourt, dribbling the ball toward the basket for an apparent layup. Out of nowhere races a defender who catches up with and accidentally undercuts your player. You see that your player is not getting up and seems to be in pain. What do you do?

No coach wants to see players get hurt. But injury remains a reality of sport participation; consequently, you must be prepared to provide first aid when injuries occur and to protect yourself against unjustified lawsuits. Fortunately, coaches can institute many preventive measures to reduce the risk. In this chapter, we describe steps you can take to prevent injuries, first aid and emergency responses for when injuries occur, and your legal responsibilities as a coach.

Game Plan for Safety

You can't prevent all injuries from happening, but you can take preventive measures that give your players the best possible chance for injury-free participation. To help you create the safest possible environment for your players, we'll explore what you can do in these areas:

- Preseason physical examinations
- Physical conditioning
- Equipment and facilities inspection
- Player matchups and inherent risks
- Proper supervision and record keeping
- Environmental conditions

Preseason Physical Examination

We recommend that your players have a physical examination before participating in basketball. The exam should address the most likely areas of medical concern and identify youngsters at high risk. We also suggest that you have players' parents or guardians sign a participation agreement form (this will be discussed in more detail later in this chapter) and an informed consent form to allow their children to be treated in case of an emergency. For a sample form, please see "Informed Consent Form" in appendix A on page 137.

Physical Conditioning

Players need to be in shape (or get in shape) to play the game at the level expected. They must have adequate cardiorespiratory fitness and muscular fitness.

Cardiorespiratory fitness involves the body's ability to use oxygen and fuels efficiently to power muscle contractions. As players get in better shape, their bodies are able to more efficiently deliver oxygen to fuel muscles and carry off carbon dioxides and other wastes. Basketball requires lots of running and exertion; most players will be moving nearly continuously and making short bursts throughout a game. Youngsters who aren't as fit as their peers often overextend in trying to keep up, which can result in light-headedness, nausea, fatigue, and potential injury.

> **Coaching Tip**
> Younger players may not be aware of when they need a break for water and a short rest; therefore, you need to work breaks into your practice schedules. It is also a good idea to have water available at all times during the practice session. This will eliminate the need for long water breaks during practice.

Try to remember that the players' goals are to participate, learn, and have fun. Therefore, you must keep the players active, attentive, and involved with every phase of practice. If you do, they will attain higher levels of cardiorespiratory fitness as the season progresses simply by taking part in practice. However, you should watch closely for signs of low cardiorespiratory fitness; don't let your players do much until they're fit. You might privately counsel youngsters who appear overly winded, suggesting that they train outside of practice (under proper supervision) to increase their fitness.

Muscular fitness encompasses strength, muscular endurance, power, speed, and flexibility. This type of fitness is affected by physical maturity, as well as strength training and other types of training. Your players will likely exhibit a relatively wide range of muscular fitness. Those who have greater muscular fitness will be able to run faster and jump higher. They will also sustain fewer muscular injuries, and any injuries that do occur will tend to be minor. And in case of injury, recovery is faster in those with higher levels of muscular fitness.

Two other components of fitness and injury prevention are the warm-up and the cool-down. Although young bodies are generally very limber, they can become tight through inactivity. The warm-up should address each muscle group and elevate the heart rate in preparation for strenuous activity. Players should warm up for 5 to 10 minutes using a combination of light running, jumping, and stretching. As practice winds down, slow players' heart rates with an easy jog or walk. Then have the players stretch for 5 minutes to help prevent tight muscles before the next practice or game.

Facilities and Equipment Inspection

Another way to prevent injuries is to regularly examine the court on which your players practice and play. Remove hazards, report conditions you cannot remedy, and request maintenance as necessary. If unsafe conditions exist, you should either make adaptations to prevent risk to your players' safety or stop the practice or game until safe conditions have been restored. You can also prevent injuries by checking the quality and fit of uniforms, practice attire, and any protective equipment used by your players. Refer to the "Facilities and Equipment Checklist" in appendix A (on page 136) to help guide you in verifying that facilities and equipment are safe.

Player Matchups and Inherent Risks

We recommend that you group teams in 2-year age increments if possible. You'll encounter fewer mismatches in physical maturation with narrow age ranges. Even so, two 12-year-old boys might differ by 90 pounds in weight, a foot in height, and 3 or 4 years in emotional and intellectual maturity. This presents dangers for the less mature. Whenever possible, you should match players against opponents of similar size and physical maturity. Such an approach gives smaller, less mature youngsters a better chance to succeed and avoid injury while providing more mature players with a greater challenge. Closely supervise games so that the more mature do not put the less mature at undue risk.

Coaching Tip

If your players vary largely in size, you should consider installing a rule that does not allow players to double-team or steal the ball from a dribbler during practices. This may help prevent bigger players from overpowering smaller players and stealing the ball at every opportunity.

Although proper matching helps protect you from certain liability concerns, you must also warn players of the inherent risks involved in playing basketball, because "failure to warn" is one of the most successful arguments in lawsuits against coaches. So, thoroughly explain the inherent risks of basketball, and make sure each player knows, understands, and appreciates those risks. Some of these inherent risks were outlined in chapter 1; you can learn more about them by talking with your league administrators.

The preseason parent-orientation meeting is a good opportunity to explain the risks of the sport to both parents and players. It is also a good time to have both the players and their parents sign a participation agreement form or waiver releasing you from liability should an injury occur. You should work with your league when creating these forms or waivers, and the forms should be reviewed by legal counsel before presentation. These forms or waivers do not relieve you of responsibility for your players' well-being, but they are recommended by lawyers and may help you in the event of a lawsuit.

Proper Supervision and Record Keeping

To ensure players' safety, you must provide both general supervision and specific supervision. *General supervision* means that you are in the area of activity so that you can see and hear what is happening. You should be

- on the court and in position to supervise the players even before the formal practice begins,

- immediately accessible to the activity and able to oversee the entire activity,
- alert to conditions that may be dangerous to players and ready to take action to protect players,
- able to react immediately and appropriately to emergencies, and
- present on the court until the last player has been picked up after the practice or game.

Specific supervision is the direct supervision of an activity at practice. For example, you should provide specific supervision when you teach new skills and should continue it until your players understand the requirements of the activity, the risks involved, and their own ability to perform in light of these risks. You must also provide specific supervision when you notice players breaking rules or a change in the condition of your players. As a general rule, the more dangerous the activity, the more specific the supervision required. This suggests that more specific supervision is required with younger and less experienced players.

As part of your supervisory duties, you are expected to foresee potentially dangerous situations and to be positioned to help prevent them. This requires that you know basketball well, especially the rules that are intended to provide for safety. Prohibit dangerous horseplay, and hold training sessions only under safe weather conditions (as discussed in "Environmental Conditions"). These specific supervisory activities, applied consistently, will make the play environment safer for your players and will help protect you from liability if a mishap occurs.

> **Coaching Tip**
> Supervision is very important to ensure that the basketball skills you teach are performed in a consistent manner. The more adults that can help supervise the skills, the better the players can learn and perform those skills.

For further protection, keep records of your season plans, practice plans, and players' injuries. Season and practice plans come in handy when you need evidence that players have been taught certain skills, whereas accurate, detailed injury report forms offer protection against unfounded lawsuits. Ask for these forms from your sponsoring organization (see page 138 in appendix A for a sample injury report form), and hold onto these records for several years so that an "old basketball injury" of a former player doesn't come back to haunt you.

Environmental Conditions

Even though basketball is a game that is typically played indoors, the versatility of the game allows it to be played outside as well. Many players will practice on their own at outside courts, and many camps and youth practices are held outside because gym space is often not available. Most health problems

Coaching Tip

Encourage players to drink plenty of water before, during, and after practice. Water makes up 45 to 65 percent of a youngster's body weight, and even a small amount of water loss can cause severe consequences in the body's systems. It doesn't have to be hot and humid for players to become dehydrated, nor is thirst an accurate indicator. In fact, by the time players are aware of their thirst, they are long overdue for a drink.

caused by environmental factors are related to excessive heat or cold, although you should also consider other environmental factors such as severe weather and air pollution. A little thought about the potential problems and a little effort to ensure adequate protection for your players will prevent most serious emergencies related to environmental conditions.

Heat .

On hot, humid days the body has difficulty cooling itself. Because the air is already saturated with water vapor (humidity), sweat doesn't evaporate as easily. Therefore, body sweat is a less effective cooling agent, and the body retains extra heat. Hot, humid environments put players at risk of heat exhaustion and heatstroke (see more on these in "Serious Injuries" on pages 43-45). And if *you* think it's hot or humid, it's worse for the kids, not only because they're more active, but also because kids under the age of 12 have more difficulty regulating their body temperature than adults do. To provide for players' safety in hot or humid conditions, take the following preventive measures. Table 4.1 lists some warm-weather precautions for different temperatures.

- Monitor weather conditions and adjust training sessions accordingly.
- Acclimatize players to exercising in high heat and humidity. Athletes can adjust to high heat and humidity in 7 to 10 days. During this period, hold practices at low to moderate activity levels and give the players fluid breaks every 20 minutes.
- Switch to light clothing. Players should wear shorts and white T-shirts.
- Identify and monitor players who are prone to heat illness. This would include players who are overweight, heavily muscled, or out of shape and players who work excessively hard or have suffered previous heat

Table 4.1   Warm-Weather Precautions

Temperature (°F)	Humidity	Precautions
80-90	<70%	Monitor players prone to heat illness.
80-90	>70%	5-minute rest after 30 minutes of practice.
90-100	<70%	5-minute rest after 30 minutes of practice.
90-100	>70%	Short practices in evenings or early morning.

illness. Closely monitor these players and give them fluid breaks every 15 to 20 minutes.

- Make sure players replace fluids lost through sweat. Encourage players to drink 17 to 20 ounces of fluid 2 to 3 hours before each practice or game, to drink 7 to 10 ounces every 20 minutes during and after each practice and game, and to drink 16 to 24 ounces of fluid for every pound lost. Fluids such as water and sports drinks are preferable during games and practices (suggested intakes are based on NATA [National Athletic Trainers' Association] recommendations).

- Encourage players to replenish electrolytes, such as sodium (salt) and potassium, that are lost through sweat. The best way to replace these nutrients—as well as others such as carbohydrates (energy) and protein (muscle building)—is by eating a balanced diet. Experts say that additional salt intake may be helpful during the most intense training periods in the heat.

Cold

When a person is exposed to cold weather, the body temperature starts to drop below normal. To counteract this, the body shivers to create heat and reduces blood flow to the extremities to conserve heat in the core of the body. But no matter how effective the body's natural heating mechanism is, the body will better withstand cold temperatures if it is prepared to handle them. To reduce the risk of cold-related illnesses, make sure players wear appropriate protective clothing, and keep the players active to maintain body heat. Also monitor the windchill factor because it can drastically affect the severity of players' responses to the weather. The windchill factor index is shown in table 4.2.

Table 4.2　Windchill Factor Index

		Temperature (°F)								
		0	5	10	15	20	25	30	35	40
		Flesh may freeze within one minute								
Wind speed (mph)	40	-55	-45	-35	-30	-20	-15	-5	0	10
	35	-50	-40	-35	-30	-20	-10	-5	5	10
	30	-50	-40	-30	-25	-20	-10	0	5	10
	25	-45	-35	-30	-20	-15	-5	0	10	15
	20	-35	-30	-25	-15	-10	0	5	10	20
	15	-30	-25	-20	-10	-5	0	10	15	25
	10	-20	-15	-10	0	5	10	15	20	30
	5	-5	0	5	10	15	20	25	30	35

Windchill temperature (°F)

Severe Weather

Severe weather refers to a host of potential dangers, including lightning storms, tornadoes, hail storms, and heavy rains. Lightning, when playing basketball outside, is of special concern because it can come up quickly and can cause great harm or even kill. For each 5-second count from the flash of lightning to the bang of thunder, lightning is one mile away. A flash-bang of 10 seconds means lightning is two miles away; a flash-bang of 15 seconds indicates lightning is three miles away. It is recommended that a practice or competition should be stopped for the day if lightning is three miles away or closer (15 seconds or less from flash to bang). In addition to these suggestions, your school, league, or state association may also have rules that you will want to consider in severe weather.

Safe places to take cover when lightning strikes include fully enclosed metal vehicles with the windows up, enclosed buildings, and low ground (under cover of bushes, if possible). It's not safe to be near metal objects such as flag poles, fences, light poles, and metal bleachers. Also avoid trees, water, and open fields.

You should cancel practice when under either a tornado watch or warning. If you are practicing or competing when a tornado is nearby, you should get inside a building if possible. If you cannot get into a building, lie in a ditch or other low-lying area or crouch near a strong building, using your arms to protect your head and neck.

The keys to handling severe weather are caution and prudence. Don't try to get that last 10 minutes of practice in if lightning is on the horizon. Don't continue to play in heavy rain. Many storms can strike both quickly and ferociously. Respect the weather and play it safe.

Air Pollution

Poor air quality and smog can present real dangers to your players. Both short- and long-term lung damage are possible from breathing polluted air. Although it's true that participating in clean air is not possible in many areas, restricting activity is recommended when the air quality ratings are lower than moderate or when there is a smog alert in your area. Your local health department or air quality control board can inform you of the air quality ratings for your area and when restricting activities is recommended.

Responding to Players' Injuries

No matter how good and thorough your prevention program is, injuries most likely will occur. When injury does strike, chances are you will be the one in charge. The severity and nature of the injury will determine how actively involved you'll be in treating it. But regardless of how seriously a player is hurt, it is your responsibility to know what steps to take. Therefore, you must be prepared to take appropriate action and provide basic emergency care when an injury occurs.

Being Prepared

Being prepared to provide basic emergency care involves many things, including being trained in cardiopulmonary resuscitation (CPR) and first aid, having a first aid kit on hand, and having an emergency plan.

First Aid Kit

A well-stocked first aid kit should include the following:

- Antibacterial soap or wipes
- Arm sling
- Athletic tape—one and a half inches wide
- Bandage scissors
- Bandage strips—assorted sizes
- Blood spill kit
- Cell phone
- Contact lens case
- Cotton swabs
- Elastic wraps—three inches, four inches, and six inches
- Emergency blanket
- Examination gloves—latex free
- Eye patch
- Foam rubber—one-eighth inch, one-fourth inch, and one-half inch
- Insect sting kit
- List of emergency phone numbers
- Mirror
- Moleskin
- Nail clippers
- Oral thermometer (to determine if a player has a fever caused by illness)
- Penlight
- Petroleum jelly
- Plastic bags for crushed ice
- Prewrap (underwrap for tape)
- Rescue breathing or CPR face mask
- Safety glasses (for first aiders)
- Safety pins
- Saline solution for eyes
- Sterile gauze pads—three-inch and four-inch squares (preferably nonstick)
- Sterile gauze rolls
- Sunscreen—sun protection factor (SPF) 30 or greater
- Tape adherent and tape remover
- Tongue depressors
- Tooth saver kit
- Triangular bandages
- Tweezers

Adapted, by permission, from M. Flegel, 2004, *Sport first aid*, 3rd ed. (Champaign, IL: Human Kinetics), 20.

CPR and First Aid Training

We recommend that all coaches receive CPR and first aid training from a nationally recognized organization such as the National Safety Council, the American Heart Association, the American Red Cross, or the American Sport Education Program (ASEP). You should be certified based on a practical test and a written test of knowledge. CPR training should include pediatric and adult basic life support and obstructed airway procedures.

Emergency Plan

An emergency plan is the final step in being prepared to take appropriate action for severe or serious injuries. The plan calls for three steps:

1. *Evaluate the injured player.*

   Use your CPR and first aid training to guide you. Be sure to keep these certifications up to date. Practice your skills frequently to keep them fresh and ready to use if and when you need them.

2. *Call the appropriate medical personnel.*

   If possible, delegate the responsibility of seeking medical help to another calm and responsible adult who attends all practices and games. Write out a list of emergency phone numbers and keep it with you at practices and games. Include the following phone numbers:

   - Rescue unit
   - Hospital
   - Physician
   - Police
   - Fire department

   Take each player's emergency information to every practice and game (see "Emergency Information Card" in appendix A on page 139). This information includes the person to contact in case of an emergency, what types of medications the player is using, what types of drugs the player is allergic to, and so on.

   Give an emergency response card (see "Emergency Response Card" in appendix A on page 140) to the contact person calling for emergency assistance. Having this information ready should help the contact person remain calm. You must also complete an injury report form (see page 138 in appendix A) and keep it on file for any injury that occurs.

3. *Provide first aid.*

   If medical personnel are not on hand at the time of the injury, you should provide first aid care to the extent of your qualifications. Again, although your CPR and first aid training will guide you, you must remember the following:

- Do not move the injured player if the injury is to the head, neck, or back; if a large joint (ankle, knee, elbow, shoulder) is dislocated; or if the pelvis, a rib, or an arm or leg is fractured.
- Calm the injured player and keep others away from her as much as possible.
- Evaluate whether the player's breathing has stopped or is irregular, and if necessary, clear the airway with your fingers.
- Administer artificial respiration if the player's breathing has stopped. Administer CPR if the player's circulation has stopped.
- Remain with the player until medical personnel arrive.

Emergency Steps

You must have a clear, well-rehearsed emergency action plan. You want to be sure you are prepared in case of an emergency because every second counts. Your emergency plan should follow this sequence:

1. Check the player's level of consciousness.

2. Send a contact person to call the appropriate medical personnel and to call the player's parents.

3. Send someone to wait for the rescue team and direct them to the injured player.

4. Assess the injury.

5. Administer first aid.

6. Assist emergency medical personnel in preparing the player for transportation to a medical facility.

7. Appoint someone to go with the player if the parents are not available. This person should be responsible, calm, and familiar with the player. Assistant coaches or parents are best for this job.

8. Complete an injury report form while the incident is fresh in your mind (see page 138 in appendix A).

Taking Appropriate Action

Proper CPR and first aid training, a well-stocked first aid kit, and an emergency plan help prepare you to take appropriate action when an injury occurs. In the previous section, we mentioned the importance of providing first aid to the extent of your qualifications. Don't "play doctor" with injuries; sort out

Coaching Tip

You shouldn't let a fear of acquired immune deficiency syndrome (AIDS) and other communicable diseases stop you from helping a player. You are only at risk if you allow contaminated blood to come in contact with an open wound on your body, so the examination gloves that you wear will protect you from AIDS if one of your players carries this disease. Check with your sport director, your league, or the Centers for Disease Control and Prevention (CDC) for more information about protecting yourself and your participants from AIDS.

minor injuries that you can treat from those that need medical attention. Now let's look at taking the appropriate action for minor injuries and more serious injuries.

Minor Injuries

Although no injury seems minor to the person experiencing it, most injuries are neither life threatening nor severe enough to restrict participation. When these injuries occur, you can take an active role in their initial treatment.

Scrapes and Cuts   When one of your players has an open wound, the first thing you should do is put on a pair of disposable latex-free examination gloves or some other effective blood barrier. Then follow these four steps:

1. Stop the bleeding by applying direct pressure with a clean dressing to the wound and elevating it. The player may be able to apply this pressure while you put on your gloves. Do not remove the dressing if it becomes soaked with blood. Instead, place an additional dressing on top of the one already in place. If bleeding continues, elevate the injured area above the heart and maintain pressure.

2. Cleanse the wound thoroughly once the bleeding is controlled. A good rinsing with a forceful stream of water, and perhaps light scrubbing with soap, will help prevent infection.

3. Protect the wound with sterile gauze or a bandage strip. If the player continues to participate, apply protective padding over the injured area.

4. Remove and dispose of gloves carefully to prevent you or anyone else from coming into contact with blood.

For bloody noses not associated with serious facial injury, have the player sit and lean slightly forward. Then pinch the player's nostrils shut. If the bleeding continues after several minutes, or if the player has a history of nosebleeds, seek medical assistance.

Strains and Sprains   The physical demands of playing basketball often result in injury to the muscles or tendons (strains) or to the ligaments (sprains). When your players suffer minor strains or sprains, you should immediately apply the PRICE method of injury care:

P Protect the player and the injured body part from further danger or trauma.

R Rest the injured area to avoid further damage and foster healing.

I Ice the area to reduce swelling and pain.

C Compress the area by securing an ice bag in place with an elastic wrap.

E Elevate the injury above heart level to keep the blood from pooling in the area.

Bumps and Bruises   Inevitably, basketball players make contact with each other and with the ground. If the force applied to a body part at impact is great enough, a bump or bruise will result. Many players continue playing with such sore spots, but if the bump or bruise is large and painful, you should take appropriate action. Again, use the PRICE method for injury care and monitor the injury. If swelling, discoloration, and pain have lessened, the player may resume participation with protective padding; if not, the player should be examined by a physician.

Serious Injuries

Head, neck, and back injuries; fractures; and injuries that cause a player to lose consciousness are among a class of injuries that you cannot and should not try to treat yourself. In these cases, you should follow the emergency plan outlined on pages 40-41 . We do want to examine more closely, however, your role in preventing heat cramps, heat exhaustion, and heatstroke. Additionally, please refer to figure 4.1 for an illustrative example of the signs and symptoms associated with heat exhaustion and heatstroke.

Heat Cramps   Tough practices combined with heat stress and substantial fluid loss from sweating can provoke muscle cramps commonly known as *heat cramps*. Cramping is most common during the early part of the season when the weather is the hottest and the players may be the least adapted to heat. The cramp, a severe tightening of the muscle, can drop players and prevent continued play. Dehydration, electrolyte loss, and fatigue are the contributing factors. The immediate treatment is to have the player cool off and slowly stretch the contracted muscle. The player may return to play later that same day or the next day provided the cramp doesn't cause a muscle strain.

Heat Exhaustion   Heat exhaustion is a shocklike condition caused by dehydration and electrolyte depletion. Symptoms include headache, nausea,

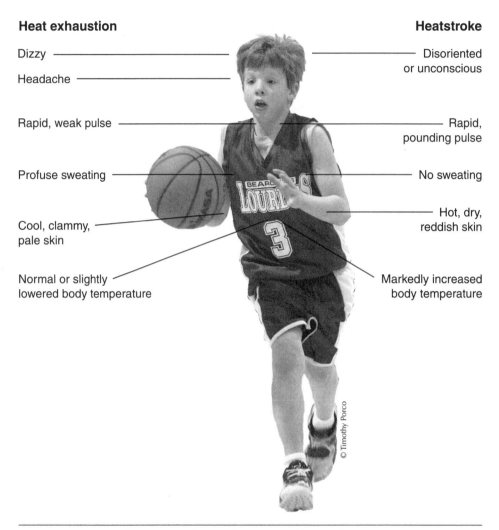

Heat exhaustion

Dizzy

Headache

Rapid, weak pulse

Profuse sweating

Cool, clammy, pale skin

Normal or slightly lowered body temperature

Heatstroke

Disoriented or unconscious

Rapid, pounding pulse

No sweating

Hot, dry, reddish skin

Markedly increased body temperature

© Timothy Porco

Figure 4.1   Signs and symptoms of heat exhaustion and heatstroke.

dizziness, chills, fatigue, and extreme thirst. Profuse sweating is a key sign of heat exhaustion. Other signs include pale, cool, and clammy skin; rapid, weak pulse; loss of coordination; and dilated pupils.

A player suffering from heat exhaustion should rest in a cool, shaded area; drink cool fluids, particularly those containing electrolytes; and apply ice to the neck, back, or abdomen to help cool the body. If you believe a player has heat exhaustion, seek medical attention. Under no conditions should the player return to activity that day or before he regains all the weight lost through sweat. If the player has to see a physician, the player shouldn't return to the team until he has a written release from the physician.

Heatstroke   Heatstroke is a life-threatening condition in which the body stops sweating and body temperature rises dangerously high. It occurs when dehydration causes a malfunction in the body's temperature control center in the brain. Symptoms include the feeling of being extremely hot, nausea, confusion, irritability, and fatigue. Signs include hot, dry, and flushed or red skin (this is a key sign); lack of sweat; rapid pulse; rapid breathing; constricted pupils; vomiting; diarrhea; and possibly seizures, unconsciousness, or respiratory or cardiac arrest.

If you suspect that a player is suffering from heatstroke, send for emergency medical assistance immediately and cool the player as quickly as possible. Remove excess clothing and equipment from the player, and cool the player's body with cool, wet towels, by pouring cool water over the player, or by placing the player in a cold-water bath. Apply ice packs to the armpits, neck, back, abdomen, and between the legs. If the player is conscious, give her cool fluids to drink. If the player is unconscious, place the player on her side to allow fluids and vomit to drain from the mouth. A player who has suffered heatstroke may not return to the team until she has a written release from a physician.

Protecting Yourself

When one of your players is injured, naturally your first concern is the player's well-being. Your feelings for youngsters, after all, are what made you decide to coach. Unfortunately, you must also consider something else: Can you be held liable for the injury?

From a legal standpoint, a coach must fulfill nine duties. We've discussed all but planning in this chapter (planning is discussed in chapters 5 and 10). The following is a summary of your legal duties:

1. Provide a safe environment.
2. Properly plan the activity.
3. Provide adequate and proper equipment.
4. Match players appropriately.
5. Warn of inherent risks in the sport.
6. Supervise the activity closely.
7. Evaluate players for injury or incapacitation.
8. Know emergency procedures, CPR, and first aid.
9. Keep adequate records.

In addition to fulfilling these nine legal duties, you should check your organization's insurance coverage and your own insurance coverage to make sure these policies will properly protect you from liability.

Making Practices
Fun and Practical

In the past, we have placed too much emphasis on the learning of skills and not enough on learning how to play skillfully—that is, how to use those skills in competition. The games approach, in contrast to the traditional approach, emphasizes learning what to do first, then how to do it. Moreover, the games approach lets kids discover what to do in the game, not by your telling them, but by their experiencing it. It is a guided discovery method of teaching that empowers your kids to solve the problems that arise in the game, which is a large part of the fun in learning.

On the surface, it would seem to make sense to introduce basketball using the traditional approach—by first teaching the basic skills of the sport and then the tactics of the game—but this approach has been shown to have disadvantages. First, it teaches the skills of the sport out of the context of the game. Kids may learn to shoot, pass, and dribble the ball, but they find it difficult to use these skills in the real game. This is because they do not yet understand the fundamental tactics of basketball and do not appreciate how best to use their new-found skills. Second, learning skills by doing drills outside of the context of the game is downright boring. The single biggest turnoff in sports is overorganized instruction that deprives kids of their intrinsic desire to play the game.

The games approach is taught using a four-step process. These steps are as follows:

1. Play a modified game.
2. Help players understand the game.
3. Teach the skills of the game.
4. Practice the skills in another game.

Step 1: Play a Modified Game

It's the first day of practice; some of the kids are eager to get started, while others are obviously apprehensive. Some have rarely dribbled a ball, most don't know the rules, and none know the positions in basketball. What do you do?

If you used the traditional approach, you would start with a quick warm-up activity, then line the players up for a simple dribbling drill and go from there. With the games approach, however, you begin by playing a modified game that is developmentally appropriate for the level of the players and also designed to focus on learning a specific part of the game.

Modifying the game emphasizes a limited number of situations in the game. This is one way you "guide" your players to discover certain tactics in the game. For instance, you can have your players play a 2v2 or 3v3 game in a half-court situation; the objective of the game is to make four passes before attempting to score. Playing the game this way forces players to think about what they have to do to keep possession of the ball.

Activities Checklist

When developing activities for your youth basketball program, here are a few questions that you should ask yourself:

- Are the activities fun?
- Are the activities organized?
- Are the players involved in the activities?
- Do the activities require the players to use creativity and decision making?
- Are the spaces used appropriate for the activities?
- Is the coach's feedback appropriate?
- Are there implications for the game?

Step 2: Help Players Understand the Game

As your players are playing a modified game, you should look for the right spot to "freeze" the action, step in, and ask questions about errors that you're seeing. When you do this, you help the players better understand the objective of the game, what they must do to achieve that objective, and also what skills they must use to achieve that objective.

Asking the right questions is a very important part of your teaching. Essentially, you'll be asking your players—often literally—"What do you need to do to succeed in this situation?" Sometimes players simply need to have more time playing the game, or you may need to modify the game further so that it is even easier for them to discover what they need to do. It may take more patience on your part, but it's a powerful way for players to learn. For example, assume your players are playing a game in which the objective is to make four passes before attempting to score, but they are having trouble doing so. Interrupt the action and ask the following questions:

- What are you supposed to do in this game?
- What does your team have to do to keep the ball for four passes in a row?
- How could you help your teammate get closer to the basket for a better shot?
- Did you acknowledge your teammate for a pass that led to your basket?
- What are some things you can do without the ball to help complete the four passes?

Coaching Tip

If your players have trouble understanding what to do, you can phrase your questions to let the players choose between one option and another. For example, if you ask them, "What's the fastest way to get the ball down the court?" and get an answer such as "Throw it," then ask, "Is it passing or dribbling?"

At first, asking the right questions might seem difficult because your players have little or no experience with the game. Or, if you've learned sport through the traditional approach, you'll be tempted to tell your players how to play the game rather than wasting time asking questions. When using the games approach, however, you must resist this powerful temptation to tell your players what to do.

Instead, through the modified game and skillful questioning on your part, your players should come to the realization on their own that accurate passing and receiving skills are essential to their success in controlling the ball. Just as important, rather than telling them what the critical skills are, you led them to this discovery, which is a crucial part of the games approach.

Step 3: Teach the Skills of the Game

Only when your players recognize the skills they need to be successful in the game do you want to teach the specific skills through focused activities (i.e., activities consisting of the skills needed to be successful in a specific game situation). This is when you use a more traditional approach to teaching sport skills, the IDEA approach, which we will describe in chapter 6. This type of teaching breaks down the skills of the game. It should be implemented early in the season so that players can begin attaining skill, which will make games more fun.

Step 4: Practice the Skills in Another Game

As a coach, you want your players to experience success as they're learning skills, and the best way for them to experience this success early on is for you to create an advantage for the players. Once the players have practiced the skill, as outlined in step 3, you can then put them in another game situation—this time a lopsided game (e.g., 3v1, 3v2). The idea is that this makes it more likely that, for instance, in a 3v1 game, your three offensive players will be able to make four passes before attempting to score.

We recommend first using even-sided games (e.g., 2v2, 3v3, 4v4) and then introducing lopsided games. This sequence enables you to first introduce your players to a situation similar to what they will experience in competition and to let them discover the challenges they face in performing the necessary skill. Then you teach them the skill, have them practice it, and put them back in another game—this time using a lopsided advantage to give them a greater chance of experiencing success.

As players improve their skills, however, you may not need to use lopsided games. A three-on-one advantage, for example, will eventually become too easy and won't challenge your players to hone their skills. When this time comes, you can lessen the advantage, or you may even decide that they're ready to practice the skill in even-sided competition. The key is to set up situations where your players experience success yet are challenged in doing so. This will take careful monitoring on your part, but having kids play lopsided games as they are learning skills is a very effective way of helping them learn and improve.

And that's the games approach. Your players will get to play more in practice, and once they learn how the skills fit into their performance and enjoyment of the game, they'll be more motivated to work on those skills, which will help them to be successful.

Coaching Tip
You may want to make a habit of ending each practice with a fun activity so that the players leave practice with a positive frame of mind. In turn, the players will look forward to returning to the next practice.

6

Teaching and Shaping Skills

Coaching basketball is about teaching kids how to play the game by teaching them skills, fitness, and values. It's also about "coaching" players before, during, and after games. Teaching and coaching are closely related, but there are important differences. In this chapter, we focus on principles of teaching, especially on teaching technical and tactical skills. But these principles apply to teaching values and fitness concepts as well. Armed with these principles, you will be able to design effective and efficient practices and will understand how to deal with misbehavior. Then you will be able to teach the skills and plays necessary to be successful in basketball (which are outlined in chapters 7 and 8).

Teaching Basketball Skills

Many people believe that the only qualification needed for teaching a skill is to have performed it. Although it's helpful to have performed it, teaching it successfully requires much more than that. And even if you haven't performed the skill before, you can still learn to teach successfully with the useful acronym IDEA:

I   Introduce the skill.

D   Demonstrate the skill.

E   Explain the skill.

A   Attend to players practicing the skill.

Introduce the Skill

Players, especially those who are young and inexperienced, need to know what skill they are learning and why they are learning it. You should therefore follow these three steps every time you introduce a skill to your players:

1. Get your players' attention.
2. Name the skill.
3. Explain the importance of the skill.

Get Your Players' Attention

Because youngsters are easily distracted, you should do something to get their attention. Some coaches use interesting news items or stories. Others use jokes. And still others simply project enthusiasm to get their players to listen. Whatever method you use, speak slightly above your normal volume and look your players in the eye when you speak.

Also, position players so they can see and hear you. Arrange the players in two or three evenly spaced rows, facing you. (Make sure they aren't looking into the sun or at a distracting activity.) Then ask whether all of them can see you before you begin to speak.

Name the Skill

More than one common name may exist for the skill you are introducing, but you should decide as a staff before the start of the season which one you'll use (and then stick with it). This will help prevent confusion and enhance communication among your players. When you introduce the new skill, call it by name several times so that the players automatically correlate the name with the skill in later discussions.

> **Coaching Tip**
> You may want to write out in detail each skill you will teach. This can clarify what you will say and how you will demonstrate and teach each skill to your players.

Explain the Importance of the Skill

As Rainer Martens, the founder of the American Sport Education Program (ASEP), has said, "The most difficult aspect of coaching is this: Coaches must learn to let athletes learn. Sport skills should be taught so they have meaning to the child, not just meaning to the coach." Although the importance of a skill may be apparent to you, your players may be less able to see how the skill will help them become better basketball players. Offer them a reason for learning the skill, and describe how the skill relates to more advanced skills.

Demonstrate the Skill

The demonstration step is the most important part of teaching sport skills to players who may never have done anything closely resembling the skill. They need a picture, not just words. They need to see how the skill is performed. If you are unable to perform the skill correctly, ask an assistant coach, one of your players, or someone more skilled to perform the demonstration.

These tips will help make your demonstrations more effective:

- Use correct form.
- Demonstrate the skill several times.
- Slow the action, if possible, during one or two performances so players can see every movement involved in the skill.
- Perform the skill at different angles so your players can get a full perspective of it.
- Demonstrate the skill with both the right and left arms and legs.

Explain the Skill

Players learn more effectively when they're given a brief explanation of the skill along with the demonstration. You should use simple terms and, if possible, relate the skill to previously learned skills. Ask your players whether they understand your description. A good technique is to ask the team to repeat your explanation. Ask questions such as "What are you going to do first?" and "Then what?" If players look confused or uncertain, you should repeat your explanation and demonstration. If possible, use different words so your players get a chance to try to understand the skill from a different perspective.

Complex skills are often better understood when they are explained in more manageable parts. For instance, if you want to teach your players how to perform the crossover dribble, you might take the following steps:

1. Show them a correct performance of the entire skill, and explain its function in basketball.

2. Break down the skill and point out its component parts to your players.

3. Have players perform each of the component skills you have already taught them, such as controlling the dribble at knee level, dribbling with the head up to see the rim, and protecting the ball with the body and the nondribbling hand.

4. After players have demonstrated their ability to perform the separate parts of the skill in sequence, reexplain the entire skill.

5. Have players practice the skill in gamelike conditions.

Young players have short attention spans, and a long demonstration or explanation of a skill may cause them to lose focus. Therefore, you should spend no more than a few minutes altogether on the introduction, demonstration, and explanation phases. Then involve the players in drills or games that call on them to perform the skill.

How to Properly Run Your Drills

Before running a drill that teaches technique, you should do the following:

- Name the drill.
- Explain the skill or skills to be taught.
- Position the players correctly.
- Explain what the drill will accomplish.
- State the command that will start the drill.
- Identify the signal that will end the drill, such as a whistle.

Once the drill has been introduced and repeated a few times in this manner, you will find that merely calling out the name of the drill is sufficient; your players will automatically line up in the proper position to run the drill and practice the skill.

Attend to Players Practicing the Skill

If the skill you selected was within your players' capabilities and you have done an effective job of introducing, demonstrating, and explaining it, your players should be ready to attempt the skill. Some players, especially those in younger age groups, may need to be physically guided through the movements during their first few attempts. Walking unsure players through the skill in this way will help them gain confidence to perform the skill on their own.

You should look at the entire skill and then break it down into components. For example, when teaching the skill of shooting the basketball, you can use the acronym "BEEF" to break down the skill into components that will help your players learn the proper technique for shooting the ball:

B   Balance (position the shooting foot slightly ahead of the other foot for balance)

E   Elbow (the elbow should be in a straight line with the shooting foot and knee)

E   Eyes (the eyes should be focused on the rim and never watch the ball in flight)

F   Follow-through (after the release, the thumb of the shooting hand should be pointed down)

Your teaching duties, though, don't end when all your players have demonstrated that they understand how to perform a skill. In fact, your teaching role is just beginning as you help your players improve their skills. A significant part of your teaching consists of closely observing the hit-and-miss trial performances of your players. You will shape players' skills by detecting errors and correcting them using positive feedback. Keep in mind that your positive feedback will have a great influence on your players' motivation to practice and improve their performances.

Remember, too, that some players may need individual instruction. So set aside a time before, during, or after practice to give individual help.

Helping Players Improve Skills

After you have successfully taught your players the fundamentals of a skill, your focus will be on helping them improve the skill. Players learn skills and improve on them at different rates, so don't get frustrated if progress seems slow. Instead, help them improve by shaping their skills and detecting and correcting errors.

Shaping Players' Skills

One of your principal teaching duties is to reward positive effort or behavior—in terms of successful skill execution—when you see it. A player makes a good pass in practice, and you immediately say, "That's the way to extend! Good follow-through!" This, plus a smile and a "thumbs-up" gesture, go a long way toward reinforcing that technique in that player. However, sometimes you may have a long dry spell before you see correct techniques to reinforce. It's difficult to reward players when they don't execute skills correctly. How can you shape their skills if this is the case?

Shaping skills takes practice on your players' part and patience on yours. Expect your players to make errors. Telling the player who made the great pass that she did a good job doesn't ensure that she'll have the same success next time. Seeing inconsistency in your players' technique can be frustrating. It's even more challenging to stay positive when your players repeatedly perform a skill incorrectly or have a lack of enthusiasm for learning. It can certainly be frustrating to see players who seemingly don't heed your advice and continue to make the same mistakes.

Although it is normal to get frustrated sometimes when teaching skills, part of successful coaching is controlling this frustration. Instead of getting upset, use these six guidelines for shaping skills:

1. *Think small initially.*

   Reward the first signs of behavior that approximate what you want. Then reward closer and closer approximations of the desired behavior. In short, use your reward power to shape the behavior you seek.

2. *Break skills into small steps.*

   For instance, in learning to dribble, one of your players does well in keeping the ball close to his body, but he's bouncing the ball too high and doesn't effectively shield it from defenders. Reinforce the correct technique of keeping the ball close, and teach him how to dribble at knee level. Once he masters this, you can focus on getting him to shield the ball from defenders.

3. *Develop one component of a skill at a time.*

   Don't try to shape two components of a skill at once. For example, in rebounding, players must first block their opponents out, then go for the ball. Players should focus first on one aspect (blocking out by putting their back against their opponent's chest and creating a wide base), then on the other (putting their hands up and going for the ball). Players who have problems mastering a skill often do so because they're trying to improve two or more components at once. You should help these players to isolate a single component.

4. *Use reinforcement only occasionally, for the best examples.*

By focusing only on the best examples, you will help players continue to improve once they've mastered the basics. Using occasional reinforcement during practice allows players to have more contact time with the ball rather than having to constantly stop and listen to the coach. Basketball skills are best learned through a lot of repetition, such as drills, and the coach needs to make the best use of team practice time by allowing the players as much time with the ball as possible.

5. *Relax your reward standards.*

As players focus on mastering a new skill or attempt to integrate it with other skills, their old, well-learned skills may temporarily degenerate, and you may need to relax your expectations. For example, a player has learned how to shoot the ball and is now learning how to combine that skill with the dribble. While learning to combine the two skills and getting the timing down, the player's shooting may be poor. A similar degeneration of ball skills may occur during growth spurts while the coordination of muscles, tendons, and ligaments catches up to the growth of bones.

6. *Go back to the basics.*

If, however, a well-learned skill degenerates for long, you may need to restore it by going back to the basics. For example, you may need to go back to the "BEEF" method of shooting technique to help restore the player's skill.

> **Coaching Tip**
> For older age groups or players with advanced skills, coaches can ask players to "self-coach." With the proper guidance and a positive team environment, young players can think about how they perform a skill and how they might be able to perform it better. Self-coaching is best done at practice, where a player can experiment with learning new skills.

Detecting and Correcting Errors

Good coaches recognize that players make two types of errors: learning errors and performance errors. Learning errors are ones that occur because players don't know how to perform a skill; that is, they have not yet developed the correct motor pattern in the brain to perform a particular skill. Performance errors are made not because players don't know how to execute the skill, but because they have made a mistake in executing what they do know. There is no easy way to know whether a player is making learning or performance errors; part of the art of coaching is being able to sort out which type of error each mistake is.

The process of helping your players correct errors begins with you observing and evaluating their performances to determine if the mistakes are learning or performance errors. You should carefully watch your players to see if they routinely make the errors in both practice and game settings, or if the errors tend to occur only in game settings. If the latter is the case, then your players are making performance errors. For performance errors, you need to look for the reasons your players are not performing as well as they know how; perhaps they are nervous, or maybe they get distracted by the game setting. If the mistakes are learning errors, then you need to help them learn the skill, which is the focus of this section.

When correcting learning errors, there is no substitute for knowledge of the skills. The better you understand a skill—not only how it is performed correctly but also what causes learning errors—the more helpful you will be in correcting your players' mistakes.

One of the most common coaching mistakes is to provide inaccurate feedback and advice on how to correct errors. Don't rush into error correction; wrong feedback or poor advice will hurt the learning process more than no feedback or advice at all. If you are uncertain about the cause of the problem or how to correct it, you should continue to observe and analyze until you are more sure. As a rule, you should see the error repeated several times before attempting to correct it.

> **Coaching Tip**
> Correcting errors is part of what coaching is all about, but don't get caught up correcting errors all the time. Give positive feedback when a player makes small steps toward progress, but give them some freedom to figure it out on their own.

Correct One Error at a Time

Suppose Jill, one of your forwards, is having trouble with her shooting. She's doing some things well, but you notice that she's extending her arm on too flat a trajectory, resulting in too low an arc, and she's not squaring up to face the basket on all of her shots. What do you do?

First, decide which error to correct first, because players learn more effectively when they attempt to correct one error at a time. Determine whether one error is causing the other; if so, have the player correct that error first, because it may eliminate the other error. In Jill's case, however, neither error is causing the other. In such cases, players should correct the error that is easiest to correct and will bring the greatest improvement when remedied. For Jill, this probably means squaring up to the basket. Correcting this error will likely motivate her to correct the other error.

Use Positive Feedback to Correct Errors

The positive approach to correcting errors includes emphasizing what to do instead of what not to do. Use compliments, praise, rewards, and encouragement to correct errors. Acknowledge correct performance as well as efforts to improve. By using positive feedback, you can help your players feel good about themselves and promote a strong desire to achieve.

When you're working with one player at a time, the positive approach to correcting errors includes four steps:

1. *Praise effort and correct performance.*

   Praise the player for trying to perform a skill correctly and for performing any parts of it correctly. Praise the player immediately after he performs the skill, if possible. Keep the praise simple: "Good try," "Way to hustle," "Good extension," or "That's the way to follow through." You can also use nonverbal feedback, such as smiling, clapping your hands, or any facial or body expression that shows approval.

   Make sure you're sincere with your praise. Don't indicate that a player's effort was good when it wasn't. Usually a player knows when he has made a sincere effort to perform the skill correctly and perceives undeserved praise for what it is—untruthful feedback to make him feel good. Likewise, don't indicate that a player's performance was correct when it wasn't.

2. *Give simple and precise feedback to correct errors.*

   Don't burden a player with a long or detailed explanation of how to correct an error. Give just enough feedback so that the player can correct one error at a time. Before giving feedback, recognize that some players readily accept it immediately after the error; others will respond better if you slightly delay the correction.

   For errors that are complicated to explain and difficult to correct, you should try the following:

   - Explain and demonstrate what the player should have done. Do not demonstrate what the player did wrong.

   - Explain the causes of the error, if it isn't already obvious.

   - Explain why you are recommending the correction you have selected, if it's not obvious.

3. *Make sure the player understands your feedback.*

   If the player doesn't understand your feedback, she won't be able to correct the error. Ask the player to repeat the feedback and to explain and demonstrate how it will be used. If the player can't do this, you should be patient and present your feedback again. Then have the player repeat the feedback after you're finished.

4. *Provide an environment that motivates the player to improve.*

   Your players won't always be able to correct their errors immediately, even if they do understand your feedback. Encourage them to "hang tough" and stick with it when corrections are difficult or when players seem discouraged. For more difficult corrections, you should remind players that it will take time, and that the improvement will happen only if they work at it. Encourage those players with little self-confidence.

Saying something like, "You were dribbling at a much better speed today; with practice, you'll be able to keep the ball closer to you and shield it from defenders," can motivate a player to continue to refine his dribbling skills.

Other players may be very self-motivated and need little help from you in this area; with them you can practically ignore step 4 when correcting an error. Although motivation comes from within, you should try to provide an environment of positive instruction and encouragement to help your players improve.

A final note on correcting errors: Team sports such as basketball provide unique challenges in this endeavor. How do you provide individual feedback in a group setting using a positive approach? Instead of yelling across the court to correct an error (and embarrass the player), you can substitute for the player who erred, and then make the correction on the sideline. This type of feedback has several advantages:

- The player will be more receptive to the one-on-one feedback.
- The other players are still active and still practicing skills, and they are unable to hear your discussion.
- Because the rest of the team is still playing, you'll feel compelled to make your comments simple and concise—which is more helpful to the player.

This doesn't mean you can't use the team setting to give specific, positive feedback. You can do so to emphasize correct group and individual performances. Use this team feedback approach only for positive statements, though. Keep any negative feedback for individual discussions.

Dealing With Misbehavior

Players will misbehave at times; it's only natural. Following are two ways you can respond to misbehavior: through extinction or discipline.

Extinction

Ignoring a misbehavior—neither rewarding nor disciplining it—is called *extinction*. This can be effective under certain circumstances. In some situations, disciplining young people's misbehavior only encourages them to act up further because of the recognition they get. Ignoring misbehavior teaches youngsters that it is not worth your attention.

Sometimes, though, you cannot wait for a behavior to fizzle out. When players cause danger to themselves or others, or disrupt the activities of others, you need to take immediate action. Tell the offending player that the behavior must stop and that discipline will follow if it doesn't. If the player doesn't stop misbehaving after the warning, you should use discipline.

Extinction also doesn't work well when a misbehavior is self-rewarding. For example, you may be able to keep from grimacing if a youngster kicks you in the shin, but even so, that youngster still knows you were hurt. Therein lies the reward. In these circumstances, it is also necessary to discipline the player for the undesirable behavior.

Extinction works best in situations where players are seeking recognition through mischievous behaviors, clowning, or grandstanding. Usually, if you are patient, their failure to get your attention will cause the behavior to disappear. However, you must be alert that you don't extinguish desirable behavior. When youngsters do something well, they expect to be positively reinforced. Not rewarding them will likely cause them to discontinue the desired behavior.

> **Coaching Tip**
> At the start of practice, you should let players know your expectations for their behavior during practice. Announce any rules you have for practice, such as "When the whistle blows, there will be no bouncing of the basketball." This helps the players realize their boundaries and your expectations.

Discipline

Some educators say we should never discipline young people, but should only reinforce their positive behaviors. They argue that discipline does not work, that it creates hostility, and that it sometimes develops avoidance behaviors that may be more unwholesome than the original problem behavior. It is true that discipline does not always work and that it can create problems when used ineffectively, but when used appropriately, discipline is effective in eliminating undesirable behaviors without creating other undesirable consequences. You must use discipline, because it is impossible to guide players through positive reinforcement and extinction alone. Discipline is part of the positive approach when these guidelines are followed:

- Discipline players in a corrective way to help them improve now and in the future. Don't discipline to retaliate and make yourself feel better.
- Impose discipline in an impersonal way when players break team rules or otherwise misbehave. Shouting at or scolding players indicates that your attitude is one of revenge.
- Once a good rule has been agreed on, ensure that players who violate it experience the unpleasant consequences of their misbehavior. Don't wave discipline threateningly over their heads. Just do it, but warn a player once before disciplining.
- Be consistent in administering discipline.
- Don't discipline using consequences that may cause you guilt. If you can't think of an appropriate consequence right away, tell the player you will talk with her after you think about it. You might consider involving the player in designing a consequence.

- Once the discipline is completed, don't make players feel that they are "in the doghouse." Always make them feel that they're valued members of the team.
- Make sure that what you think is discipline isn't perceived by the player as a positive reinforcement; for instance, keeping a player out of doing a certain activity or portion of the training session may be just what the player wanted.
- Never discipline players for making errors when they are playing.
- Never use physical activity—running laps or doing push-ups—as discipline. To do so only causes players to resent physical activity, something we want them to learn to enjoy throughout their lives.
- Use discipline sparingly. Constant discipline and criticism cause players to turn their interests elsewhere and to resent you as well.

Coaching Offense

This chapter focuses on the offensive techniques and tactics that players need to learn in order to perform effectively in youth basketball games. Remember to use the IDEA approach to teaching skills: introduce, demonstrate, and explain the skill, and attend to players as they practice the skill (see page 54 in chapter 6). This chapter also ties directly into the season and practice plans in chapter 10, describing the technical skills and team tactics that you'll teach at the practices outlined there. If you aren't familiar with basketball skills, you may find it helpful to watch a video so you can see the skills performed correctly. Also, the Coaching Youth Basketball Online Course offered by the American Sport Education Program (ASEP) can help you further understand these skills (you can take this course by going to www.ASEP.com).

The information in this book is limited to basketball basics. As your players advance in their skills, you will need to advance your knowledge as a coach. You can do this by learning from your experiences, watching and talking with more experienced coaches, and studying resources on advanced skills.

Offensive Technical Skills

Figure 7.1   Ready position for offense.

The offensive technical skills you will teach your players include ready position, footwork, dribbling, passing and catching, shooting, and rebounding. Mastering these skills will allow your players to better execute your offensive tactics—or plays—during the game. These basic technical skills serve as the foundation for playing basketball well at all levels. Basketball players practice these techniques at every practice, from youth basketball to the pros.

Ready Position

The ready position—sometimes called *basketball position*—is the position from which all offensive moves should be made. From this ready position, the offensive player can perform any offensive skill—shooting, running, passing, dribbling, screening, pivoting, or jumping—in a very efficient manner because the player is ready to move quickly in any direction. In the ready position, the feet are shoulder-width apart or wider, and the knees are bent and out from the body (see figure 7.1). The hands and arms are above the waist to make the player seem as big as possible.

Triple-Threat Position

The triple-threat position is a version of the ready position where the player squares up to the basket whenever she receives the ball. This position allows the offensive player to see the entire court. It also puts the player in a position where she can make one of three choices—to shoot, pass, or dribble—without letting the defense know which she is going to use.

When assuming the triple-threat position, the player should be square to the basket with her body facing the basket and the defender so that she is in a good position to shoot, pass, or drive to the right or the left. The player should hold the ball to the side near the hip, with elbows out; the player's hands should always remain in shooting position, with one hand behind the ball and the other hand on the side, allowing her to shoot the ball quickly and in rhythm, if necessary. The shooting foot, which is the foot on the same side as the shooting hand, should be positioned slightly ahead of the other foot so that the player is in balance to take a shot if she chooses to do so (see photo). To keep a defender off guard, a player in the triple-threat position should move the ball, keeping the ball close to the chest and never lower than the waist.

Offensive Footwork

Good footwork is important for both offense and defense, but offensive players have an advantage over defenders because they know what moves they are going to make and when. Offensive players use footwork to fake defenders off balance, move off screens, cut to the basket, prevent charging into a defender, and to elude a blockout when going for a rebound. We'll explore four types of basic footwork—cuts, jump stops, pivots, and jab steps.

Cuts

Offensive players use cuts to change direction quickly (while staying in balance) and "lose" their opponents in order to get open for passes or shots. Defenders will find it difficult to keep up if they are unable to respond correctly to the cut.

A player executes a cut by planting one foot on the court at the end of a slightly shortened stride, then pushing off that foot to shift his momentum in another direction. For example, if a player wants to cut to the right, he will first push off with the left foot (see figure 7.2a). Then, he will turn the unplanted foot in the direction he wants to go and will lead with that leg as he bursts in the new direction (see figure 7.2b). When cutting, a player should bend the knees to lower his center of gravity and provide explosiveness from the legs. After cutting, he should always strive to get his lead hand up as a target for a pass.

a   b

Figure 7.2   Proper body positioning for a cut to the right.

Three types of cuts that offensive players use to get open are V-cuts, L-cuts, and backdoor cuts.

V-Cut   A V-cut is used by an offensive player to get open at the wing when the defensive player has a foot and hand in the passing lane and is trying to deny a pass to the offensive player. The ideal place for the offensive player to receive the ball is at the wing position, which is even with the free throw line halfway between the free throw lane and the sideline. The V-cut should be the offensive player's first option in getting to this position because it is the easiest cut to use and the quickest method to get open. To execute a V-cut, the offensive player moves from the wing position and takes her defender to the basket. She then plants the foot closest to the basket and pushes off toward the wing position to receive the ball (see figure 7.3a).

Coaching Tip
Younger players commonly take an arced path when cutting, or they slow down, taking short steps before the cut. You should teach your players that cuts must be hard, sharp, and explosive in order to be most effective and keep the defense on edge.

L-Cut   An L-cut is also used by an offensive player to get open at the wing when a defender has a foot and hand in the passing lane, trying to deny the pass. Again, the ideal place for the offensive player to receive the ball is at the wing position. The L-cut is used when the V-cut will not get the offensive player open to catch the ball. To execute an L-cut, the offensive player should first be in the ready position. He moves to a spot just outside the free throw lane (about even with the middle of the lane) and then takes the defensive player slowly to the elbow of the free throw line. He plants his inside foot and crosses over with the outside foot to move straight out to the wing to receive the ball (see figure 7.3b).

Backdoor Cut   A backdoor cut is used by an offensive player when a defender has a foot and hand in the passing lane to deny a pass from the outside into

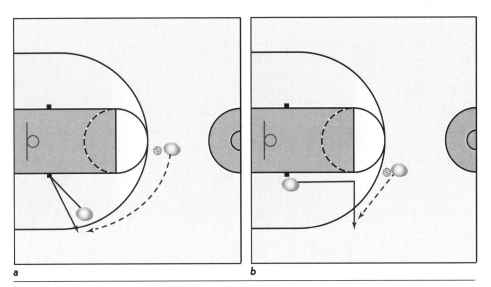

a   b

Figure 7.3   (a) V-cut and (b) L-cut.

(continued)

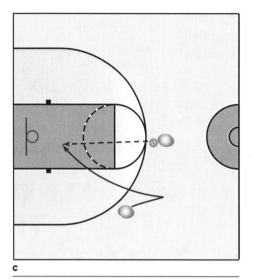

c

Figure 7.3   *(continued) (c)* Backdoor cut.

the wing position. This cut is used to reduce the pressure at the wing. Since the defender is denying the pass to the wing, the offensive player must execute a backdoor cut toward the basket to get open. To execute a backdoor cut, the player should move to the outside by taking her defensive player a step above the free throw line. She then plants the foot closest to the half-court line and quickly cuts behind her defender and toward the basket (see figure 7.3c).

Two-Ball Cutting Drill

Players line up in groups of five at the top of the key on both ends of the court. The second and third players in line each have a ball. The first player in line executes a cut (V-cut, L-cut, or backdoor cut) to get the ball, which the second player in line will pass. Once the player receives the pass, he turns and shoots. He then rebounds his own shot, takes a position at the end of the line, and passes the ball up the line. The second player in line, who made the pass previously, now acts as the cutter and executes a cut to get the ball, which the third player in line will pass. Repeat in this manner for 5 to 10 minutes or until all players in line have executed a cut.

Jump Stops

A jump stop is used to stop quickly when on the run, with or without the ball. It is a necessary maneuver almost any time a pass is received at any position on the floor. The jump stop is particularly advantageous when a player receives a pass while facing away from the basket in the low-post area, which is anywhere within eight feet of the basket, because it will allow the player to use either foot as her pivot foot; this gives the offensive player an advantage.

To jump stop, a player on the run quickly stops her body under control by allowing both feet to hit the floor at the same time and assuming the ready position, with the feet shoulder-width apart, the knees flexed, and her weight shifted slightly forward to the balls of the feet (see figure 7.4 *a* and *b*). The player's arms should be in a position above the waist, ready to receive the ball, and the head should be up and positioned over the waist. If a player tends to

a   b

Figure 7.4 Jump stop.

lose her balance when making the jump stop, you should teach her to shift her weight to the back of the feet, with the head back and in line with the body (loss of balance is commonly a result of the player's head being positioned too far forward in front of the feet).

After completing the jump stop, the player can then choose either foot as a pivot foot, but she may not change that pivot foot while in possession of the ball (see "Pivots" for more information).

Four-Line Jump Stop Drill

Players divide into four groups and line up along the baseline. When the coach blows the whistle, the first players in line sprint forward. The coach blows a second whistle (after approximately five or six steps by the players), and the players use a jump stop to stop quickly with both feet simultaneously hitting the floor. The coach blows another whistle, and the next players in line begin. Repeat in this manner until all players have reached the opposite baseline.

Pivots

A pivot takes place when one foot is lifted off the floor while the other foot is used to turn the body. When players receive the ball, they can use either a front or back pivot to protect the ball from the defense, to pass to a teammate, or to make a move to the basket. A pivot can be made while on the run with or without the ball, for example, when performing a crossover dribble or a V-cut. A pivot can also be made when a player is stationary, such as when a player uses it to gain an advantage.

A front pivot is when the turn of the pivot moves forward. Players should use a front pivot in situations when they are facing the basket because it will allow them to keep their eyes on the basket and not turn their back to their teammates. To execute a front pivot, the player must assume a ready position—with the feet shoulder-width apart and the knees bent—and maintain this position throughout the pivot. The player then turns his body by lifting one foot and moving his body forward. The player should keep his weight on the ball of the pivot foot; that is, the foot that remains on the court.

A back pivot is when the turn of the pivot moves backward. Players use a back pivot when a defender is guarding them very closely and they cannot make the front pivot without committing a violation or foul. Players will often use the back pivot in an effort to avoid contact with the defensive player. To execute a back pivot, the player must assume a ready position—with the feet shoulder-width apart and the knees bent—and maintain this position throughout the pivot. The player takes a drop step, also called a *reverse turn*, by allowing his back to lead the way and lifting one foot and then dropping it back. The player should keep his weight on the ball of the pivot foot (the foot that remains on the court).

It is important to note that once a pivot foot is chosen, the player cannot lift or slide that foot, because doing so would become a violation called *traveling*. However, when attempting a pass or shot, the player may lift the designated pivot foot—providing the player releases the ball before the pivot foot again hits the floor.

Dribble-Pivot-Pass Drill

Players divide into four groups and line up along the sideline. The first players in line each have a ball, and on the coach's command, they move forward, dribbling twice, and jump stop. After the jump stop, the players execute a pivot (either front or back), pass the ball to the next player in line, and return to the end of the line. Repeat until all players have had a turn.

Jab Steps

A jab step—also called a *drive step*—is a short, 8- to 10-inch step made straight toward the defender with the nonpivot foot. A player will use a jab step to create space between herself and the defensive player.

To execute a jab step, the player catches the ball from a teammate and immediately assumes the ready position and squares up to the basket (see figure 7.5a). The player's weight should be on the pivot foot, and the player takes a short step directly at the defensive player with the other foot (see figure 7.5b).

a   b

Figure 7.5   Jab step.

Jab Stepping Drill

Players divide into three groups and line up at the top of the key. The first players in line each have a ball, and on the coach's command, they push the ball out three or four feet in front of them. The players take their first step with the nonshooting foot, which will be the pivot foot, and with the shooting foot, they take a jab step. After the jab step, the players shoot the ball, rebound it, and pass it to the next player in their lines. Repeat until all players have had a turn.

Dribbling

Simply stated, dribbling is used to maintain possession of the ball while moving by bouncing the ball on the floor. At the start of the dribble, the ball

Coaching Tip

Teach your players that a pass travels much faster than a dribble, so before dribbling, a player should always first look for an opportunity to pass to an open teammate.

must leave the hand before the player lifts her pivot foot from the floor, as discussed in "Pivots" on page 72, and the player may not touch the ball simultaneously with both hands while dribbling or allow it to come to a rest in her hand.

Dribbling is an integral part of the sport of basketball and is vital to individual and team play; however, it is also the most misused fundamental skill in the game. Excessive dribbling with no purpose can quickly destroy teamwork and the morale of your team. For example, if a player dribbles too much, teammates will tend not to move or react, making the defense's job much easier. When learning the skill of dribbling, young players must first understand that all dribbling must have a purpose, such as to advance the ball up the court or to the basket, or to make the passing angle better to get a pass to an open teammate. Players must also keep their dribble in motion until a shot or pass is available; picking up—or "killing"—the dribble in a poor position without an option of a pass or a shot often results in a turnover.

When dribbling, your players should first maintain the ready position, keeping the knees bent and the rear down, and establish a feel for the ball with the pads of the fingers (see figure 7.6). Players should work to keep the dribble under control by always bouncing the ball below waist height and even lower when being guarded closely by a defender. The ball should be kept close to the body, and the player should protect the dribble from the defender with the nondribbling hand and arm. The head should always be up so that the player can "see the rim" and be aware of what is happening on the rest of the court, such as the location of defenders and teammates.

It is helpful for players to learn at a young age how to dribble with both hands. The ability to dribble with the weak hand as well as the strong hand is one key in advancing a player's skill level. When a player can move effectively in either direction with a dribble, this forces the

Figure 7.6 Proper body positioning for a dribble.

defender to play in a more squared up position to the dribbler and allows the offensive player more freedom to go in either direction. Young players should also work on their ability to change speed and direction while dribbling, because this makes it more difficult for the defender to anticipate the offensive player's next move.

There are many types of dribbles that players can use; however, we're going to take a look at two of the most common dribbles that are used in youth basketball—the power dribble and the crossover dribble. We also discuss dribbling techniques that players should use when driving to the basket (see "Driving to the Basket" on page 77).

Coaching Tip

When dribbling, players should strive to stay in the middle of the court and stay away from the sidelines and corners. It is much more difficult for the defense to trap or double-team a dribbler in the middle of the floor. Players should visualize the sideline as another defender and continually work to stay away from it.

Dribbling Don'ts

Dribbling can be a very effective weapon to use in many situations, but as we have learned, it is often an overused offensive skill. Following are a few key "don'ts" to teach your players:

- Don't dribble with the head down, as players will not be able to see teammates open for a pass.
- Don't use only one hand when dribbling. Players should be able to dribble with either hand.
- Don't dribble the ball out from the body in traffic because it will be much harder to protect the ball from defensive players.
- Don't automatically start dribbling after receiving a pass. After receiving the pass, players should first square up to the basket in a triple-threat position and look to see what shooting or passing options are available to them.
- Don't pick up or stop the dribble until a clear shot or pass option becomes available.
- Don't dribble into a crowd—the ball is more likely to be stolen.
- Don't try to get fancy when good fundamental dribbling will do the job.
- Don't hesitate. Players should be assertive and confident when dribbling the ball.

Dribbling Line Drill

Players divide into eight groups and line up across from each other, four lines on each side, along the sidelines on both sides of the court. The first players in each line have a ball, and on the coach's command, they dribble forward toward the middle of the court, using a type of dribble specified by the coach. When the players meet in the middle, they execute a crossover dribble (or another dribble specified by the coach) and continue to the opposite sideline, giving the ball to the next player in line. Repeat until all players have had a turn.

Power Dribble

A power dribble is a hard dribble that allows the player to make a move in a close space and free himself from tight defense. The power dribble is most often used on a drive to the basket, but it can also be used to get out of a congested area, such as when a player secures a rebound but is surrounded by defenders with no open teammate to pass to.

The power dribble calls on many of the same fundamentals as described previously for dribbling, but it combines them with an explosive first step toward the basket or in the direction the player is moving. The ball is put down hard on the floor with both hands, almost as if it is being thrown, as the offensive player takes several quick steps with the dribble, typically to the left or right of the defensive player.

As with all dribbles, players should be taught to keep the head up and "see the rim" so that they are aware of what is happening on the court. Additionally, the player should dribble off the finger pads with fingertip control, flexing the wrist and fingers to impart force to the ball without pumping the arm.

Crossover Dribble

The crossover dribble is a type of dribble where the dribbler actually crosses the ball in front of the defensive player in order to make a change in direction (left or right), typically from the strong hand to the weak hand. A player should use a crossover dribble when overplayed by the defender, meaning that the defender is trying to restrict the direction that the offensive player may go. The crossover dribble is used in the open court on a fast break or to create space between the dribbler and the defender for a drive to the basket or for a better shot.

To execute the crossover dribble, the player should first plant the foot on the side of the body that he is dribbling on. The player then crosses the ball in front, switching the dribble from one hand to the other on the bounce, while crossing the leg over in front of the defender in the direction that he wants to go. After changing direction, the player should remember to get his nondribbling hand up for protection.

Driving to the Basket

When the ball handler finds an opening, she will make a drive to the basket. To execute this drive properly, the player should take a longer step—called a *drive step*—in a straight line to the basket, close to her defender, while keeping her weight on the pivot foot (see photo). The drive step should move past the defender's lead foot, cutting off the defender's retreat by closing the gap between the offensive player and the defender's retreat step. The offensive player then takes a long dribble with the outside hand (the hand farthest away from the defender) and makes the drive while keeping the head up and the eyes on the basket. After driving by the defender, the player should be alert for defensive help and should finish by going in strong for a layup or passing to an open teammate who can score.

Passing

Effective passing is the key to moving the ball into position to take high-percentage shots. Players pass the ball to maintain possession and create scoring opportunities. Passes should usually be short and crisp, and they should arrive above the waist and within easy reach of the receiver. Long or slow passes are likely to be stolen, and players should avoid throwing too hard or using passes that are difficult to control. Additionally, if possible, passes should be thrown to the receiver's side that is farthest from the defender.

We'll take a closer look at three types of passes: chest pass, bounce pass, and overhead pass.

Coaching Tip

Although all passers need to see their targets, more advanced players should practice seeing their targets without looking at them, by looking or faking away before passing. This will help the passer better conceal where she intends to pass the ball.

Partner Passing Drill

Players divide into groups of two and position anywhere on the court, 12 to 15 feet apart and facing each other. Each pair of players has a ball, and the players pass back and forth to their partner, using proper technique. The coach specifies the type of passes to be made. Continue for 5 to 10 minutes, depending on the age group.

Chest Pass

The chest pass is made when the ball is thrown with two hands from the passer's chest area to the receiver's chest area. Chest passes are used often because they can be made quickly and accurately from most positions on the floor.

To execute the chest pass, the player should begin in the ready position and step toward the target, extending the legs, the back, and the arms, to initiate the pass (see figure 7.7a). The pass should be started with the elbows in, and then the wrists and fingers should be forced through the ball, releasing it off the first and second fingers of both hands to give the ball backspin and direc-

a   b

Figure 7.7   Chest pass.

tion (see figure 7.7b). To get good backspin on the ball, the player should follow through with the fingers pointed at the target, palms facing out, and with the thumb of both hands pointed down.

Bounce Pass

It is sometimes easier for a passer to get the ball to a teammate by bouncing the ball once on the court before it reaches the receiver. For example, if a defender is guarding a player with both hands overhead, this may prevent a pass being made through the air to a teammate. Players should use bounce passes when they are closely guarded and do not have the space to extend their arms for a chest pass.

Coaching Tip

Often, a player's strong hand tends to dominate on a pass, forcing the ball in one direction or another versus straight ahead. Players should focus on forcing the weak hand through the ball in order to place an equal distribution of force on the ball and keep it moving straight ahead on the pass.

To execute the bounce pass, the player should first assume the ready position, with the head up and the ball held in both hands near one hip to protect the ball from the defender (see figure 7.8a). The player should step toward the target and snap the thumbs down and together on the release, as shown in figure 7.8b, to impart backspin on the ball, which will slow the

a   b

Figure 7.8 Bounce pass.

pass down a little as it hits the floor. The player should make the pass at waist level and aim to bounce the ball on the court about two-thirds of the way between herself and the receiver so that the receiver is able to catch it at waist level.

Overhead Pass

An overhead pass is used when a player is closely guarded and is forced to pass over a defender—for example, when making an outlet pass to start a fast break or a lob pass to a player cutting backdoor to the basket. The overhead pass is also an option for feeding the low post.

To execute the overhead pass, the player should start in the ready position, holding the ball above the forehead with the elbows in and flexed at about 90 degrees (see figure 7.9a). The player should be careful not to bring the ball back behind the head, because from this position, it takes longer to make the pass, and it is easier for a defender to come in from behind and make a steal. The player then steps in the direction of the target and extends the legs and back (see figure 7.9b), quickly passing the ball by extending the arms, flexing

a   b

Figure 7.9   Overhead pass.

the wrists and fingers, and releasing the ball off the first and second fingers of both hands. The player follows through with the fingers pointing at the target and the palms facing down.

Catching

Even the best passes are of little value if they aren't caught, and sloppy receiving technique is often the cause of turnovers and missed scoring opportunities.

To receive a pass properly, the player should first show a target to the passer by putting an arm up or out to the side and call for the ball (see figure 7.10a). She should then move to meet the pass—stepping toward the ball, not away—and watch the ball into her hands (see figure 7.10b). The player's hands should be relaxed—with palms facing the passer and thumbs together in a "W" position—and should "give" with the ball as it is caught.

When possible, players should come to a jump stop after receiving a pass with their feet positioned shoulder-width apart in ready position. From this position, players should pivot to face the basket, looking for an open teammate, a shot, or a lane to dribble the ball to the basket.

a   b

Figure 7.10   Catching a pass.

Two-Line Pass and Catch Drill

Players divide into two groups and line up on the court, approximately 12 to 15 feet apart, facing each other. The first player in one line has a ball, and on the coach's command of "left," "right," or "both," the first player in the other line raises the appropriate hand (or both hands) to act as the passer's target. Once the pass is caught, the two players take a position at the end of the opposite line. Repeat until all players have had a turn.

Shooting

Most players love the chance to put the basketball through the hoop and will be highly motivated to learn proper shooting technique. However, many players spend hours shooting the basketball but never become very good shooters because they practice shots that they never take in game competition. After your players learn the fundamentals of the shot, you should make sure that they practice shooting under game conditions.

Players should first learn how to select high-percentage shots only, in other words, shots that are likely to go in. Obviously, the closer the player is to the basket when the shot is attempted, the better the chance that the shot will go in. Other factors that determine a high-percentage shot include the defensive pressure, the position of the shooter, the team offense, and the time and score of the game. High-percentage opportunities for a shot also vary depending on the player's shooting skill and the position that the player plays on the team.

When shooting, players should also learn to focus on a specific target, usually the rim or backboard. The middle of the rim should be the target for most shots, but when players are at a 30- to 60-degree angle from the hoop, they

Achieving Arc on the Shot

Many players tend to shoot "line drives" at the hoop, rather than achieving a proper arc on the ball when taking a shot. This arc can improve the chances of making a shot because a proper arc allows the ball to be somewhat off the mark and still go in the basket.

Arc is determined by the placement of the arm and hand during and after the shot. To achieve arc on the shot, players should shoot the ball up, then out, toward the basket. The player's shoulders should be relaxed and in a forward position. The player should move the hands closer together if they are too far apart; she should raise her shooting arm higher to provide more arc. A good way to check for proper arc is to examine the positioning of the shooting-arm elbow. The elbow should end up above eye level on the follow-through for the shot.

should sight the corner of the square on the backboard for a bank shot. If the angle is correct, using the backboard will help the ball go into the basket.

Players can shoot the ball in a variety of ways, including set and jump shots, free throws, layups, and shooting off a dribble.

Set and Jump Shots

Set shots are shots taken without a jump during the shot, such as the type of shot used for free throws. A jump shot, as the name implies, is a shot taken using a jump during the shot. Although the most common shot at higher levels of play is the jump shot, young players who lack the leg strength and coordination to spring from the floor while shooting will more often shoot set shots.

When executing the set shot, players should first square up to the basket, with the foot on the shooting-hand side positioned up to six inches in front of the other foot, creating a comfortable, balanced base of support (see figure 7.11a). The ball should lie on the finger pads of each hand, with the shooting hand behind and slightly underneath the ball and the nonshooting hand balancing the ball from the side. The player then bends the knees to get momentum for the shot—using the legs, not the arms, for power; at the same time, the player bends the shooting-arm elbow to approximately a 90-degree angle, keeping the forearm perpendicular to the floor and in front of the cocked wrist as the ball is brought up to the shooting position above the forehead (see figure 7.11b). As the legs extend, the player releases the ball

a   b

Figure 7.11   Set shot.

(continued)

by extending the elbow, bringing the wrist forward, and moving the fingers of the shooting hand up and through the ball (see figure 7.11c). The player should follow through after the release by landing on both feet, extending the shooting arm and dropping the wrist, and pointing the index finger of the shooting hand directly at the basket; the thumb on the shooting hand ends in the down position after the shot.

For a set shot, players should understand that the nonshooting arm and hand should maintain their supportive position on the side of the ball until after the release—the nonshooting hand should not be used to help push the ball to the basket. To verify proper positioning of the nonshoot-

c

Figure 7.11   Set shot *(continued)*.

ing hand, ensure that the thumb of the nonshooting hand is pointed back to the ear and not at the basket (see figure 7.12).

A jump shot is similar to the set shot except that the player aligns the ball higher at the point of release and shoots after jumping, rather than shooting with the simultaneous extension of the legs while on the floor. Also, because the player jumps first and then shoots, the upper body, arm, wrist, and fingers must generate more force.

When executing a jump shot, the movement above the waist is similar to that of the set shot. The shoot-

Figure 7.12   Positioning of the nonshooting hand for the set shot.

ing hand should be positioned behind the ball, with the elbow in line with the basket, and the nonshooting hand positioned to the side of the ball (see figure 7.13a). For the jump shot, however, the player should jump straight up off both feet—fully extending the ankles, knees, back, and shoulders—and should take the shot just before reaching the peak of the jump (see figure 7.13b). For a jump shot, the ball must be put into motion as the player is jumping in order to impart that power onto the ball. If a player releases the ball too late, the shot will most likely be short. The player should follow through on the jump shot with the shooting arm extended and the nonshooting hand in position with the thumb pointing back toward the ear.

Coaching Tip
Teach younger players the mechanics of the set shot first, and they will be able to advance to the jump shot as they increase their strength and improve their coordination.

The height of the player's jump depends on the range of the shot. On shots close to the basket when the player is closely guarded, she will have to jump higher than his defenders. On longer-range jump shots, she will usually have more time and defenders are not quite as close; therefore, the player won't have to jump as high for these shots. When using a jump shot, however, more

a   b

Figure 7.13 Jump shot.

force from the legs should be used for shooting the ball rather than for jumping high. Balance and control are more important than gaining maximum height on a jump.

Free Throws

Although the mechanics of a free throw are similar to a set shot, as we learned previously, free throw shooting requires a great deal of concentration because the shooter is by herself at the free throw line. Success in free throw shooting largely depends on the player's ability to be relaxed and confident in order to concentrate fully on the shots being taken.

Establishing a consistent rhythm and a set routine will help players achieve this relaxation and confidence. A routine, for example, can include dribbling a set number of times; checking mechanics; breathing deeply and exhaling fully; consciously relaxing the shoulders, arms, hands, and fingers; letting them drop and loosen; and so forth. Players may also use visualization techniques to mentally practice shooting the free throw and to focus on positive thoughts, such as *I'm a good shooter* and "seeing" the ball going through the basket.

Layups

The highest-percentage shot—and therefore the most desirable shot—is a layup. A layup is a one-handed shot taken within three feet of the basket. A layup is typically shot using the hand farthest from the basket in an effort to protect the ball from defenders. Teach players to use their left hand when shooting layups from the left side of the basket and their right hand when shooting from the right side of the basket.

When executing a layup, the player begins by striding from a 45- to 60-degree angle to the hoop and then planting and exploding—much like a high jumper—off the foot opposite the shooting hand. The player explodes off the planted foot straight up into the air. At the top of the jump, the player releases the ball by bringing the shooting hand, which is underneath the ball and near the shoulder, straight up toward the basket. As in the set shot, the index finger of the shooting hand should be pointed directly at the basket or the appropriate spot on the backboard.

When shooting a layup, the player should aim to shoot high off the backboard so that the ball drops in the basket. This way, even if the player is fouled on the shot, the ball will have a chance to go in.

Coaching Tip

Right-handed players are likely to find left-handed layups troublesome, and vice versa. The strength and coordination of younger players are not yet advanced enough to perform the layup easily from both sides of the basket. You can help your players learn to use the left hand on the left side of the basket, for example, by teaching them to visualize the left knee and left elbow attached with a string. As the left elbow goes up to release the ball, the left knee also comes up, and the player jumps off the right foot.

Shooting Off a Dribble

Shooting off the dribble is simply taking a shot after using a dribble to get into a better shooting position. The dribble also helps the shooter get more power into the shot than when a shot is taken directly from a pass.

When shooting off a dribble, the player should first achieve a balanced stance with the knees bent. She should pick up the ball while facing the basket in position to shoot. The player shouldn't reach for the ball but should instead pick it up in front of the shooting knee (the knee on the same side of the body as the shooting hand) as the ball bounces up. When a player is dribbling to the strong-hand side, she should jump behind her last dribble and pick the ball up in front of her shooting knee using the strong-side hand; the nonshooting hand will be positioned on the side of the ball for the shot (see figure 7.14, *a-c*). When

a

b   c

Figure 7.14   Shooting the ball from the strong-side dribble.

a player is dribbling to her weak-hand side, she will pick the ball up off the dribble with the weak-side hand and bring the ball to the shooting hand for the shot (see figure 7.15, *a* and *b*).

a   b

Figure 7.15   Shooting the ball from the weak-side dribble.

Two-Ball Shooting Drill

Players line up in two groups at the top of the key on both ends of the court. The second and third players in line each have a ball. The first player in line runs and touches the baseline and then moves to an appropriate place (the coach specifies the type of shot to be made) in order to receive a pass from the second player in line. The player catches the pass, pivots, and shoots the ball using proper form. The player rebounds his own shot, takes a position at the end of the line, and passes the ball up the line. The second player in line, who made the pass previously, now runs to the baseline and moves to an appropriate place in order to receive a pass from the third player in line. Repeat in this manner for 5 to 10 minutes or until all players in line have executed a shot.

Offensive Rebounding

An offensive rebound is a rebound secured by the offensive team when one of its own players misses a shot. Effective and successful offensive rebounding by your players adds greatly to your team's chances to score. Possession of the ball comes more often from missed shots than any other way, and a team that can control the backboard usually controls the game. More than any other basic basketball skill, the success of offensive rebounding relies largely on players' desire and courage. Good rebounders must be able to anticipate missed shots and determine how hard or how soft, and to what side of the rim, the ball will rebound. They must also know where their opponents are at all times.

When preparing to rebound a ball, the offensive player should be in the ready position with the hands above the shoulders so that he can achieve maximum height on his jump to go after the ball (see figure 7.16a). The hands and arms need to be fully extended so the player gets the ball at the peak of his jump instead of allowing the ball to come down to the player. A player should catch the rebound firmly with both hands (see figure 7.16b), and after controlling a rebound, the player should keep the ball at chin level with

a   b

Figure 7.16   Securing the rebound.   *(continued)*

c

Figure 7.16 Securing the rebound *(continued)*.

the elbows out (see figure 7.16*c*). The player must protect the ball while maintaining this stance with the ball at the chin and the elbows out, but at the same time the player must avoid swinging the elbows to draw a foul.

Offensive Rebound Drill

Players line up in a single-file line at the block on one side of the basket. The coach takes a shot, and the first player in line executes a V-cut or spin move to get into the proper position to rebound the ball at the basket. (The coach should take shots from different areas of the court to practice the rebounds for different types of shots.) Once the player gets the rebound, he passes the ball back to the coach and takes a position at the end of the line. Repeat until all players have had a turn.

Rebounding Shots From the Side

For a shot taken from the side, offensive players should be aware that the ball is likely to rebound to the opposite side of the basket. Players should not watch the ball in flight; instead, they should look for an opening on the opposite side so that they can position themselves for the rebound. The offensive player can get into offensive rebound position by taking a V-cut (discussed previously on page 68) toward the baseline in order to get inside position on the defender. The player can also use a pivot (discussed previously on page 72) to make a spin move around the defender.

Rebounding Shots From the Front

Offensive rebounding for shots taken from the front is similar to rebounding the shots from the side, except that shots taken from the front will usually rebound straight out from the rim. The offensive player can use the same tactics to get into offensive rebound position in front of the rim—taking a V-cut to get inside position on the defender or using a pivot to make a spin move around defenders.

Rebounding Free Throws

When rebounding free throws, the offensive player should line up as far up the lane as possible (in his box). When the ball hits the rim, the player should immediately step down the

> **Coaching Tip**
>
> A player should avoid reaching over an opponent when getting "boxed out" by the defense (see "Defensive Rebounding" in chapter 8) or else it is likely that a foul will be called. Emphasize the importance of jumping straight up for the rebound. By jumping vertically, not only will a player achieve great height, but she'll also avoid needless fouls.

lane hard and quick to try to beat the inside defender for the rebound. This will make it more difficult for the defensive rebounder to make contact and block out the offensive player.

Offensive Tactical Skills

Once your players understand and can properly execute the individual offensive technical skills, they can begin putting them together into offensive tactics. As you probably already know, the primary offensive objective in basketball is to move the ball effectively so that you can score. A secondary goal, then, is to maintain ball possession so that the opposing team cannot score. The following tactics will help your team accomplish these goals.

Coordinating an Offensive Attack

When coordinating your offensive attack, above all else, you must strive to maintain court balance and spacing and to provide opportunities for players to be in a position to score. The execution of these objectives differs depending on whether your team is up against a man-to-man or zone defense.

Against man-to-man defense, the most important thing for your players to learn is proper spacing so that the defenders cannot easily double-team the offensive player with the ball (see "Creating Passing Lanes" on page 92 for more information). For youth players, an offensive set that works well against man-to-man defense is one where the point guard (PG) leads the attack with the wings (W) stationed at the free throw line extended—approximately 17 feet from the basket—and the two post players (P) positioned on the free throw line blocks (see figure 7.17). When the ball is passed to a wing, the point guard screens away for the other wing, and a post player screens away for the

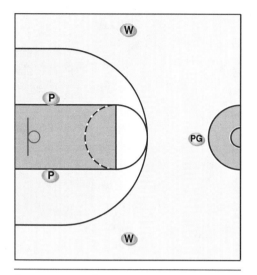

Figure 7.17   Offensive set against a man-to-man defense.

opposite post player. At times, the point guard may cut to the basket instead of setting the screen; when this happens, to regain court balance, the opposite wing will fill the front spot. The post players may also step out to the wing positions to set a ball screen and create a two-man pick-and-roll.

Against a zone defense, your players need to move quickly and strive to find positions in gaps of the defense. If players dribble the basketball between the gaps in a zone defense, this will often make two defenders cover the dribbler and leave a player open for a shot. When your team faces a 2-3 zone defense, a good offensive set to use would be a 1-3-1 set with a point guard, two wings, a high-post player, and a low-post player (see figure 7.18*a*). When facing a 1-3-1 zone defense, you should use a 2-1-2 offensive set with two guards (G), two forwards (F), and a post player in the middle. In a 2-1-2, the offense plays in the gaps of the zone defense (see figure 7.18*b*).

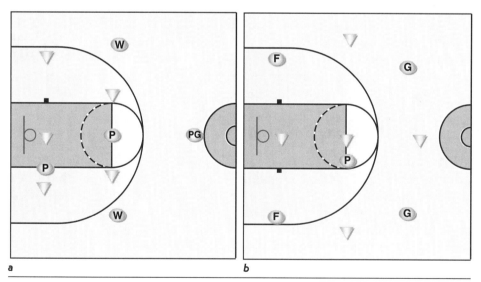

Figure 7.18   Offensive sets against a zone defense.

Creating Passing Lanes

To move the ball effectively, your team needs to move well without the ball and create passing lanes. Passing lanes are spaces or open areas where passes

Jump Balls

The jump ball occurs when both teams have equal control of the ball, as in the start of the game or overtime periods. How players are positioned for a jump ball depends on whether your team has the better chance of controlling the tip—that is, winning the jump ball. If the player jumping for you has the advantage, your team should align in an offensive formation and attempt to score off the play. If, however, it appears that the opposing team will gain possession, a defensive setup is appropriate. The jumper should tip the ball to an open spot where two teammates are next to each other without an opponent in between.

can be made between offensive players with little risk of being stolen by the defensive team. Players create passing lanes by maintaining court balance, by keeping the middle open, and by quickly moving to a vacated spot. Passing lanes can also be created by screens, which will be covered in "Setting Screens" on page 94.

Maintaining Court Balance

Court balance is necessary to allow the offense to make passes and cuts. Offensive players should start in an open formation about 12 to 15 feet apart. This spacing will make it more difficult for the defenders to double-team and will allow better opportunities for screens and cuts. Offensive players should be spaced high at the top, wide on the wing, and at the midpoint between the basket and corner on the baseline.

Keeping the Middle Open

Keeping the middle, or lane area, open is a very good offensive maneuver because it enables cutters to cut through the lane to receive the ball without much traffic. When a player cuts to the basket and doesn't receive a pass, the player should continue through and fill an open spot on the side of the court with fewer players, which is usually the opposite side from where the player came. This will keep the middle open and the floor balanced (see figure 7.19).

Additionally, players must be aware that they shouldn't stay in the post area (high, mid, or low post) for more

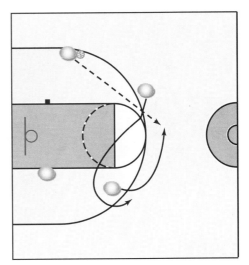

Figure 7.19 Filling an open spot on a cut.

than three counts. A violation will occur after three seconds in the lane, and the middle area will get congested if the player continues to go into the post areas.

Moving to a Vacated Spot

When a player cuts, the player who is the next player away from the cutting player should move quickly to the vacated spot. This is especially important when the player has to cut from the top position (the position at the top of the key that the point guard typically covers), because floor balance is needed so that players are in the proper position for the rebound and to stop the fast break. This top position is where the offense usually starts, depending on the offensive set being used. But as players move to various spots on the court in response to defensive movement, this point position needs to be covered by different players so that good court balance is maintained. When replacing the player at the point, the new player should swing wide above the three-point line, creating a better passing angle from the wing (see figure 7.20). The new player needs to get open for a pass at the top of the key, and if the player receives a pass, this is a good opportunity to reverse the ball to the other side of the court and make a cut to the basket.

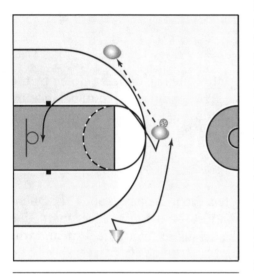

Figure 7.20   Moving to a vacated spot when a cut is taken from the point.

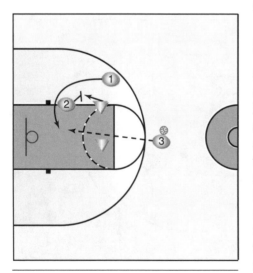

Figure 7.21   Setting a screen.

Setting Screens

Screens can be set for a player with or without the ball. They are used to help players get open for passes and shots. In figure 7.21, player 2 sets a screen—also called a *pick*—by positioning as a stationary barrier on one side of player 1's defender, thus blocking that defender's path as player 1 cuts around the screen to get open for a pass from player 3. A player will typically set a screen perpendicular to the path of the defender and will "screen away" from the ball—that is, set the screen for a player without the ball who is located on the opposite side of the court from the ball (the weak side). This way, the player for whom the screen is set will be moving toward the passer after coming off the screen.

The cutter—the player for whom the screen is set—should cut close to the screener and actually brush the screener on the way by. When playing against a good defensive team, the cutter may often be covered because defensive players will switch when a screen is set. But the screener may often be open to receive a pass after setting the screen.

When setting a screen, the player should use a wide two-footed jump stop to avoid an illegal moving screen. The player should stand erect with the feet planted shoulder-width apart and the arms down to the sides or crossed at the chest. The screener should keep the arms and knees in as the defender fights through. For more information on the technical aspects of the jump stop, see "Jump Stops" on page 70.

Running a Fast Break

The fast break usually develops after a rebound, a steal, or possibly after a basket, and it is the fastest way to make the transition from defense to offense. As soon as the defensive team gains possession, it becomes the offensive team and try to push the ball downcourt quickly before the other team can get back on defense.

To start a fast break after a basket or steal, players use a quick pass, known as an *outlet pass*, to a teammate positioned downcourt from the player in possession of the basketball. They can also dribble to start the break, but passing is the first option because it moves the ball faster. On a rebound, the outlet pass is slightly different because the teammate receiving the outlet pass will not yet be positioned downcourt. Instead, the player in possession of the ball turns to the outside of the court and looks for a guard to pass to. When the guard receives the ball, he immediately advances the ball downcourt using a dribble or another pass. If the rebounder is trapped or is in a congested area and unable to make the outlet pass, he can use one or two power dribbles up the middle and then look to pass. A point guard who sees that the rebounder is unable to make the outlet pass should come back to the rebounder to receive a short pass or handoff. The player who receives the pass will then be responsible for moving the ball to the middle of the court by either passing or dribbling. Other teammates will fill the lanes on either side as they proceed down the court. When the ball reaches the middle, the

Coaching Tip
The fast break is not started until the defensive team gains possession of the ball and then becomes the offensive team. Players must not anticipate possession and start the fast break early, because this may leave the team shorthanded on defense. Younger players often get in the habit of anticipating that a teammate will gain possession and running away from the ball to start the fast break before possession is really obtained.

player with the ball will want to get to the free throw line under control before passing to either lane for a shot or short drive.

Players should stay spread out and run at top speed under control during the fast break. The last two players down the floor are called *trailers* and are typically the bigger forward and the center (the 4 and 5 positions). They cut directly to the blocks on either side, looking for a pass from one of the outside lanes. Trailers often get passes on the blocks from the right- or left-lane cutters when the defense moves out to cover them on the wings.

Basic Offensive Plays

There are several basic offensive plays that every team should learn, including the give-and-go, the pick-and-roll, and inbounds plays.

Give-and-Go

The give-and-go is the most basic play in basketball and exemplifies what team play is all about. The name is derived from the action where one player gives (passes) the ball to a teammate and goes (cuts) to the basket, looking to receive a return pass for a layup (see figure 7.22 for an example of the movement made for a give-and-go play). By passing the ball and then moving without it, the player creates an opportunity to score on a return pass. If the player does not get open on the cut, the movement at least gives the teammate a better opportunity to initiate a one-on-one move, because the cutter's defender will be in a less advantageous position to give defensive help.

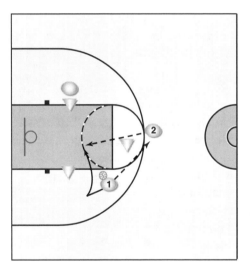

Figure 7.22   Give-and-go.

When a player is positioned at the point, she should start the give-and-go at least a step above the free throw circle. When she is on the wing, she should start the give-and-go a step above the foul line extended. The player initiates the give-and-go with a pass and then reads the defender's position before cutting to the basket. If the defender moves with the passer, continuing to guard closely, the passer should simply make a hard cut to the basket. However, if the defender drops off, moving toward the ball on the pass, the passer should set the defender up with a fake before cutting. The passer should fake by taking a step or two away from the ball, and then, as the defender moves with the passer, the passer should make a sharp cut in front of the defender toward the basket. The passer can also fake by taking a step or two toward the ball, then make a sharp cut behind the defender. This is the backdoor cut, which was discussed previously on page 69. The key is for players to read their defenders to know which type of cut will be most effective (see "Cuts" on page 68).

Pick-and-Roll

The pick-and-roll is another basic play whose name, like that of the give-and-go, comes from the action of the play. A player sets a pick (screen) for a teammate, who dribbles by it for an outside shot or a drive. The screener then rolls toward the basket, looking for a pass from the dribbler for a layup (see figure 7.23 for the movement made for a pick-and-roll play).

The player with the ball must wait until a legal pick is set before she starts the dribble. She then dribbles her defender into the screen that her teammate has set. The screener turns so she can see the dribbler and may receive a pass. The dribbler should take at least two dribbles beyond the screen to create space for the pass to the screener, who rolls to the basket.

Inbounds Plays

Inbounds plays are used to get the ball into the playing area from out of bounds—for example, after a turnover, after a made basket, or when the other team touches the ball last before it goes out of bounds. The primary goal of your inbounds plays should be to get the ball inbounds safely, to score off the inbounds play, or both.

Design most of your inbounds plays to create easy scoring opportunities when your team puts the ball in play from underneath your basket, but keep the plays simple and limit them to just a few. The key is to always have a good passer inbound the ball and for the rest of the team to cut hard to their designated spots.

Coaching Tip

After making a roll or cut, players should work to get their lead hand up for a target. This will help the passer identify where the ball should be passed. It also helps the passer know that players are looking to receive the ball as they are cutting to the basket.

Figure 7.23 Pick-and-roll.

Coaching Tip

When creating the inbounds plays for your team, consider aligning players in the same manner for each play so that your players aren't confused about where to position themselves and the defense isn't tipped off by a change in formation.

Coaching Defense

Playing defense is part instinct, part effort, and part technique. Players can improve their instincts through learning technique, practicing plays, and repetition. This chapter focuses on the defensive techniques and tactics that your players must learn to succeed in youth basketball. Again, remember to use the IDEA approach to teaching skills—introduce, demonstrate, and explain the skill, and attend to players as they practice the skill (see page 54 in chapter 6). Also, if you aren't familiar with basketball skills, you may find it helpful to watch a video so you can see the skills performed correctly.

The information in this book is limited to basketball basics. As your players advance in their skills, you will need to advance your knowledge as a coach. You can do this by learning from your experiences, watching and talking with more experienced coaches, and studying resources on advanced skills.

Defensive Technical Skills

Individual defensive skills are sometimes less appreciated than individual offensive skills, but they are just as important. To compete successfully, your players need to learn the basics of player-to-player defense.

Defensive Stance and Footwork

Figure 8.1   Basic defensive stance.

The defensive stance—commonly referred to as the *ready* or *basketball* position—is the most basic of all defensive skills. It is the positioning that defensive players should strive to maintain at all times. In the ready position, the feet are shoulder-width apart or wider, and the knees are bent and out from the body (see figure 8.1). The hands and arms are above the waist to make the player seem as big as possible so that it is much tougher for offensive players to maneuver around the defender.

From this stance, a defender must be able to slide her feet and maintain an arm's distance from her opponent who is attempting to drive or cut to the basket. Players should stand in the ready position, with the knees bent, the rear down, and the back erect; the arms should be held out above the waist. The player should move the leg nearest the intended direction about two feet to that side and then slide the other foot until the feet are once again shoulder-width apart (see figure 8.2, *a* and *b*). The player should use short, quick steps, with his weight evenly distributed on the balls of the feet. Remind the player to keep the toes pointed forward and to never cross the feet.

Coaching Tip

Younger players tend to cross their feet when attempting to move sideways on a slide. To help prevent this, you can have your players visualize holding a broomstick between their feet that will not allow the feet to cross.

a   b

Figure 8.2   Slide.

Sideline Slide Drill

Players line up perpendicular to the sideline, and on the coach's command, they assume the basic defensive stance and use slides to move across the floor. Players' arms are held out wide, and the players slap the floor on each slide to help emphasize staying low. Once all players have reached the opposite sideline, repeat the drill. Continue for three to seven minutes, depending on the age group.

Blocking or Deflecting Shots

Blocking or deflecting shots is when a defensive player jumps up and attempts to stop a shot in the air taken by the offensive team. This is a skill that not all players, especially those in younger age groups, should use because a foul is often called on this action if the defensive player cannot execute it properly. The defensive player's size, jumping ability, and the ability to properly time the jump are the main factors in determining the quality of this skill. When going for a block or a deflection, the defender should maintain the defensive stance until the ball leaves the shooter's hand. If the defender jumps too soon, the offensive player can easily draw the foul. When going for the tip or block, the defender should do so with an open hand and work to keep the ball in bounds.

Defending Shots Drill

Players divide into two groups and line up along the baseline at one end of the court. The first player in one line has a ball, and on the coach's command, this player dribbles to the basket at the opposite end of the court while the first player in the other line defends him. (The coach designates what type of shot will be taken.) When the player with the ball takes a shot, the defender uses proper technique to block or deflect the shot. The defender rebounds the ball and both players jog back up the court along the sidelines. The defender gives the ball to the first player in his original line and both take a place at the end of their original lines. Repeat until all players have had a turn at defend-. ing the shot.

Guarding

To guard a player with the ball effectively, the defensive player's stance and body positioning are the most important elements. When guarding an opponent with the ball, the defensive player should maintain the defensive stance, as described previously, with the inside hand down to help protect against the crossover dribble and the outside hand up in the passing lane to deflect a pass attempt (see figure 8.3).

When the defender is in a situation where he must turn the offensive player, such as when the offensive player is working to dribble the ball up the court, the foot positioning will change. The player must position the foot closest to the rim line at least an arm's length away from the offensive player's foot to help force the dribbler

Coaching Tip

Teach your players not to reach to the dribbler. Reaching will cause your player to get off balance and allow the dribbler to easily get around the defender. Reaching may also cause your players to foul on the dribbler.

to the baseline (see figure 8.4). In other words, the defender's foot closest to the imaginary line that runs down the center of the court from rim to rim should be placed in a position closer to this rim line than the dribbler's inside foot. This will force the dribbler to go to the outside or to the baseline. The defensive player's eyes should stay focused on the waist area of the dribbler so that she does not get faked out of position by watching the ball or the head and shoulders of the offensive player.

Figure 8.3 Defender's body positioning when guarding an opponent with the ball.

Figure 8.4 Defender's body positioning when turning an opponent with the ball.

Guarding Drill

Players divide into two groups and line up along the baseline at one end of the court. One player has the ball and acts as the offensive player and the other player acts as the defender. The offensive player moves down the court in a "zig-zag" pattern using the sideline as boundaries and dribbles the ball at half speed, so that the defender can practice proper mechanics of guarding. Once players reach the opposite baseline, the offensive player rolls the ball back to the next player in line and two more players move down the court. Repeat until all players have had a turn.

Stealing

Stealing refers to the interception of the ball when a pass is made or knocking the ball away from the dribbler. Most often, a steal occurs when a pass is made from one offensive player to another and the defender steps in the path of the pass. When attempting to steal the ball, the defensive player must anticipate where and when the pass will be thrown and get the hand in the passing lane. Stealing the ball from dribblers is often difficult because they can protect the ball using their body. Dribblers also commonly draw a foul on the defender because the defender's reach on the dribbler will often create contact with the offensive player. This also produces a poor defensive stance because the balance is poor when reaching for the ball.

Defensive Rebounding

When the offensive team shoots the ball, the defensive team will try to gain possession by rebounding the missed shot. The technique for rebounding defensively is similar to offensive rebounding in that the player must always first be in the ready position. When preparing to go for the rebound, the player's hands should be above the shoulders so that the player can achieve maximum height on the jump.

However, for defensive rebounds, players must locate their opponents first, achieve an inside position, and box out their opponent—using a front or rear pivot to get into a position between their opponent and the basket and putting their rear in contact with the opponent. This is done to ensure that the offensive player is behind the defensive player and so that the defensive player can see the flight of the ball when the shot is taken. A front pivot allows the defensive rebounder to turn while watching the offensive player move toward the rebound. A rear pivot is used to move into the path of the offensive player without the same visual contact. Encourage defenders to use whichever method gets them in position in front of the offense, sealing the offensive player away from the basket. Once contact is established with an opposing player, the defensive rebounder wants to maintain that contact until releasing to jump for the rebound.

For rebounding free throws on defense, you should place your best rebounders in the positions closest to the basket because this is where these rebounds generally go. Defenders should be in a balanced stance with the knees bent; the hands should be held above the waist in anticipation of the missed free throw. As the ball hits the rim, the defenders should step toward the free throw line to block out the offensive rebounder next to them. You should also designate a player to block out the shooter.

Defensive Rebound Drill

Players divide into four groups, with two groups positioned along the baseline on both sides of the basket and the other two groups positioned at the free throw line directly in front of the other lines. The first player in one of the lines under the basket has a ball and passes it to the first player in the line directly in front of him. This player shoots the ball and then he and the first player in the other line at the free throw line both go for the rebound. The first two players in the lines along the baseline screen out and also go for the ball. After the rebound is secured, the ball is returned to the line along the baseline where the drill was originally started and all players take a position at the end of their lines. Repeat until all players have had a turn at defensive rebounds.

Defensive Tactical Skills

Good defensive play inhibits the opponent by limiting the number of uncontested shots. Good defense not only reduces scoring opportunities for the opponent, but it also opens them to your own team. For your team to have an effective defense, your players must use not only correct defensive *technical* skills, but they must also work together with teammates to use sound defensive *tactical* skills based on the game situation.

In this section, we'll focus on several aspects of defensive tactics: coordinating a team defense, playing the post, playing on and off the ball, helping out, defending against screens, and cutting off passing lanes.

Coordinating a Team Defense

The two main types of defenses played in youth basketball are man-to-man defense and zone defense. In man-to-man defense, the defensive player is responsible for a specific offensive player, while at the same time, the player must be alert to situations where he can help his teammates and stop the offensive team from scoring. In zone defense, each defender covers an area instead of a specific offensive player—for example, in the commonly used 2-3 zone, two players cover the wings and high-post area, and three players cover the baseline and middle areas. Younger players should primarily be taught man-to-man defense. This type of defense provides them with the basic skills necessary to learn zone defense as they move into older age groups or progress in skill.

Jump Ball Strategies

The defensive jump ball situation can provide your team with a possession if played correctly. If you know that there is little chance to get the tip, then your team must attempt to force the opponent to tip the ball to the tipper's weak side—the side of the court where it would be the most difficult to tip the ball (this would be to the right and to the back for right-handed players). You should also be sure to position a player on each side of the offensive player where the tipper can most easily tip the ball. This will force the tipper to tip the ball at another player in a more difficult position.

Playing the Post

The post area refers to anywhere in the free throw lane area, with the high post being the free throw line area, the mid post being the area halfway down the lane, and the low post being the area located closest to the basket. Playing defense in the post area is different than playing defense on the perimeter (the area outside the lane). The defense will usually try to keep the ball out of the post area because it is much easier for the offensive team to score in this area. Players should defend the post offensive player based on her position and her ability. The first method is to front the offensive post player to completely deny the pass into the offensive post. To do this correctly, the help-side defensive player must be in a position to stop the lob pass over the defensive player who is in the fronting position. The second method is to play directly behind the post player. This method will allow the ball to be thrown into the post player but is intended to prevent that player from getting a shot in front of the basket. This is the best method to use when the offensive post player is not a good turnaround shooter, and it is an effective method for blocking out the offensive player. The third way is to play on one side or the other of the offensive player in a partial fronting position. This will keep the ball from entering the post and yet allow a good position for boxing out.

Playing on and off the Ball

When using a man-to-man defense, playing "off the ball" and playing "on the ball" are two basic concepts that your players must be aware of. Certain rules apply when guarding a player with the ball versus guarding players without the ball.

On the Ball

Playing "on the ball" simply refers to defending the offensive player with the ball. When playing on the ball, as the offensive player begins to dribble, the defender should react by sliding the feet and maintaining an arm's distance from the opponent. The defender should try to beat the offensive player

Figure 8.5   Guarding the dribbler.

to the spot that the player wants to reach (see figure 8.5). Moreover, if the defender can get the offensive player to stop and pick up the ball, the defender can then move closer and crowd the offensive player, blocking the passing lanes and applying extensive pressure with the arms (see figure 8.6). When playing on the ball, players should also strive to maintain focus on the opponent's midsection; if they watch the ball or their opponent's head or feet, they are likely to react to a fake that will put them out of position.

More advanced defenders can focus on four defensive strategies when playing defense on the ball:

Figure 8.6   Guarding the ball after the dribble.

- *Turning the dribbler.* Defenders who establish position a half body ahead of the dribbler can force the dribbler to turn or reverse direction. This makes it much more difficult for the dribbler to find an open teammate for the pass because the dribbler is concerned with the defender.

- *Forcing the dribbler to the sideline.* When a defensive player forces the dribbler to dribble toward the sideline, the dribbler can pass in only one direction. A defender can do this by working for position a half body to the inside of the court, with the inside foot (the one closer to the middle of the court) forward and the outside foot back. This technique limits the offensive player to one side of the court and makes the offensive team work much harder to score.

- *Forcing the dribbler to the middle.* By taking position a half body to the outside of the court, a defender can force a dribbler to the middle. This strategy will move the dribbler toward one of the defender's teammates off the ball.

- *Forcing the dribbler to use the weak hand.* By overplaying the strong hand, defenders can force the dribbler to use the weak hand. Defenders can overplay the strong hand by being a half body to the dribbler's strong-hand side.

Off the Ball

Playing "off the ball" simply means guarding an offensive player who does not have the ball. Defending an opponent without the ball is just as important as guarding a player with the ball, but it is a bit more complicated. When playing off the ball, defensive players need to apply the defensive concept of ball-you-man, as shown in figure 8.7, which simply means that a triangle is created between the offensive player with the ball, you the defender, and the offensive player that you are guarding. Defenders should also position themselves so that they can see the ball (and know if they need to come and help a teammate on a pass or drive), and they must keep track of a moving opponent (their player), who may be trying to get open to receive a pass. The closer an opponent is to the ball, the closer the defender should be to that opponent. The farther the ball is from an opponent, the farther away a defender can play that opponent and be able to give help to the teammate guarding the ball. Defenders must also be able to move quickly as the ball is passed from one offensive player to another and must be able to adjust their position in relationship

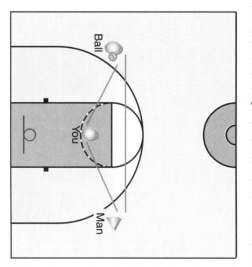

Figure 8.7   Ball-you-man positioning.

to the ball and the player they are guarding.

Denial Position

A player should use the denial position when her opponent is one pass away from the ball. The space between two offensive players where a pass can be made is called the *passing lane*. A defender wants to have an arm and leg in the passing lane when guarding a player who is one pass away (see figure 8.8). This denial position allows the defender to establish the ball-you-man relationship and discourages the offensive player with the ball from attempting a pass.

Open Position

When offensive players are two or more passes away from the ball,

Figure 8.8   Denial position.

the defensive player wants to establish an open position that still maintains the ball-you-man relationship. In the open position, the defender is farther away from the offensive player, pointing to the ball with one hand and to the opponent with the other hand (see figure 8.9). Using peripheral vision, the defender moves

Figure 8.9   Open position.

to react as the ball penetrates toward the basket (to help out on the drive) or moves into denial position if the offensive player cuts hard to receive a pass.

Defensive Techniques On and Off the Ball

Players must remember that court position and defensive stance are two of the most important techniques when playing defense regardless of whether the player they are guarding has the ball. However, there are some things that your players should be aware of when they are playing specifically on or off the ball.

On the Ball

- Am I in ready position and alert?
- Am I an arm's distance from my player (the ball handler) and able to put pressure on his ability to shoot, pass, or drive?
- Is my player close enough to attempt a good shot?
- Am I close enough to the player to prevent an easy shot?
- Am I too close, so the opponent can drive around me?
- Will a teammate be able to help me if the player beats me with the dribble?

Off the Ball

- Am I in proper position on the help side so that I can see both the ball and the player I am guarding?
- Is my player in a position to cut to the ball side and receive a pass?
- Can I get to my player if the ball is passed to him for a shot?
- Am I too close, so the opponent can make a cut to the ball?
- Am I in proper position so I can help my teammate guarding the offensive player with the ball in case he attempts to drive to the basket?

Helping Out

No matter how well your players position themselves on the court and communicate with each other on defense, an offensive player will at times be open. When this occurs, your players must know how to respond based on what kind of help is needed, and each player must be in a position to help when and where needed. For example, if one of your players spots an opponent wide open under the basket waving for a teammate to pass the ball, that defender should leave an assigned opponent who is farther from the basket and sprint to try to prevent the pass. On the other hand, if a dribbler gets by a defender and is headed for a layup, the defensive player closest to the dribbler between the dribbler and the basket should immediately move in to cut off the lane to the hoop. This can cause the offensive player to commit a charging foul, throw the ball away, or travel. The most important thing for defenders to know is where the ball is located so they can be in a position to help stop the ball, if needed. Whatever the case, the defender who has been beaten, or who loses an offensive player and sees that recovery is impossible, should shout, "Help!" All four teammates should be ready to respond if you have effectively taught them this very important defensive tactic.

On a related note, each player must also know how to properly cover gaps in the defense. Everywhere on the floor, whether it be a man-to-man defense or a zone defense, there are gaps—spaces between two defensive players—that must be covered by the defense. A good offense will try to dribble the ball in those gaps. The defenders must react quickly to this and cover the gaps by sliding the feet and trying to take the charge on the dribbler or causing a turnover.

Defending Against Screens

A screen is used by an offensive player to free up a teammate by obstructing the path of the defender. Screens can be used on defenders playing on the ball or on defenders that are guarding an offensive player away from the ball. Defensive players must be able to defend the screening action in order to stop a score. Three ways to defend against a screen are to fight over the top of the screen, to slide behind it, and to switch.

Fight Over the Top

A player should fight over the top of a screen when there is room for the defender to get between the screener and the screener's teammate. The defender whom the screen was set on should let the teammate guarding the screener know to stay with that opponent by shouting, "Through!" or "Over!" The defender being screened should work to get through the screen by first getting a foot over the screen and then the remainder of the body (see figure 8.10).

Coaching Tip
Players need to communicate and help one another when defending against screens. The defender on the opponent who is setting the screen must alert the defender being screened by calling out the direction of the screen: "Screen right!" or "Screen left!"

Figure 8.10   Fighting over the top of a screen.

Slide Behind

Sliding behind the screen should be used when guarding a poor shooter, a quick driver, or when the screen is set too far away from the basket for the offensive player to shoot the ball. When an opponent sets a screen on a player guarding a quick driver or when the action is outside the opponent's shooting range, the player being screened should slide behind the screen by moving under the opponent on the basket side, rather than on top (see figure 8.11).

Switch

When teammates are of equal size and defensive ability, the easiest defensive move against a screen is to switch opponents. As the offensive player dribbles around the screen, the defender guarding the screener will switch to guarding the dribbler, and the defender guarding the dribbler will now guard the screener. This is the best method to stop the dribbler from going to the basket; however, it does open up the court for the pass to the screener. If size and defensive ability differ, switching should be the last option because it allows the offense to take advantage of a mismatch. Players who switch should call out the screen by yelling, "Switch!" As players switch, one player must aggressively get in position to deny a pass to the cutter (the screener who rolls to the basket) while the other player gets in position on the ball side of the screener (see figure 8.12).

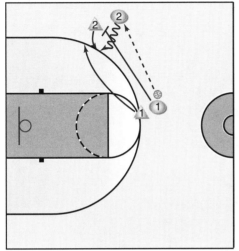

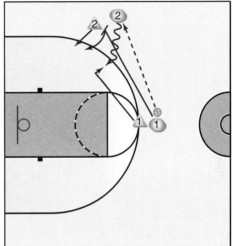

Figure 8.11   Sliding behind a screen.   **Figure 8.12**   Switching on a screen.

9

Coaching
on Game Day

Games provide the opportunity for your players to show what they've learned in practice. Just as your players' focus shifts on game days from learning and practicing to competing, your focus shifts from teaching skills to coaching players as they perform those skills in games. Of course, the game is a teaching opportunity as well, but the focus is on performing what has been learned, participating, and having fun.

In previous chapters, you learned how to teach your players techniques and tactics; in this chapter, you will learn how to coach your players as they execute those techniques and tactics in games. We provide important coaching principles that will guide you before, during, and after the game.

Before the Game

Many coaches focus on how they will coach only during the actual game, when instead preparations should begin well before the first play of the game. Ideally, a day or two before a game, you should cover several things—in addition to techniques and tactics—to prepare your players for the game. Depending on the age group you are working with, you will need to create a specific game plan for the opponent based on information that is available to you. This task will include making decisions on specific team tactics that you want to use. You should also discuss pregame particulars such as what to eat before the game, what to wear, and when to be at the gym.

Deciding Team Tactics

Some coaches burn the midnight oil as they devise a complex plan of attack. Team tactics at this level, however, don't need to be complex—especially for the younger age groups. The focus should be on consistent execution, moving the ball on offense, and playing good team defense. You should emphasize the importance of teamwork, of every player fulfilling her role on offense and defense, and of every player knowing her assignments. As you become more familiar with your team's tendencies and abilities, you can help them focus on specific tactics that will help them play better.

During the week before a game, you should inform players of the tactics that you think will work and that you plan to use in the game. Pick out several offensive sets and plays and the main defense that you want to use in the game. Try to practice these at every practice, and make certain that every player understands the plays and that

Coaching Tip

When developing your game plan, keep in mind that your players need to understand what you expect of them both offensively and defensively during the game. Be clear about this in the days leading up to a game. Take time at the beginning or end of each practice to discuss these expectations.

Creating a Game Plan

Just as you need a practice plan for what you will cover at each practice, you also need a game plan for game day. As a coach for youth basketball, your game plan will vary depending on the age group you are working with. As you begin planning and mapping out how your game days will progress, you should keep the following age-related points in mind.

Ages 6 to 8	• Encourage players to try their best. • Focus on helping players develop their individual skills for team competition. • While the use of games is important, do not spend too much time just playing games without time for proper skill instruction.
Ages 9 to 11	• The strengths and weaknesses of the opposition are of little concern at this age; the focus should be on helping your team execute the skills they have learned. • Use simple team offenses that make it easy for your players to execute the techniques and skills learned in practice. • Remind players of one offensive and one defensive aspect that they have learned, and have them focus on these aspects for the game. • Give players a starting lineup before the first game.
Ages 12 to 14	• Players should begin to focus on one or two of the opponent's strengths and weaknesses, and they should be able to take advantage of this while the game is being played. • Teams will sometimes adjust their play based on the opponent, but the main focus is still the proper execution of the techniques and skills learned in practice. • Use more complex team offenses and defenses that will take advantage of the opponent's weaknesses.

the team can run them without error. Limiting the number of plays allows you to repeat them during practice and instill in your players the confidence that they can execute the plays that will be called during the game.

Depending on the age level, experience, and knowledge of your players, you may want to let them help you determine the first offensive play or set and the defense that you will call in the game. It is the coach's role to help youngsters grow through the sport experience. Allowing player input helps your players learn the game and involves them at a planning level often reserved solely for the coach. It also gives them a feeling of ownership. Rather than just carrying out orders for the coach, they're executing the plan of attack that they helped decide. Youngsters who have a say in how they approach a task often respond with more enthusiasm and motivation.

Discussing Pregame Details

Players need to know what to do before a game, such as what they should eat on game day and when, what clothing they should wear to the game, what equipment they should bring, what time they should arrive, and how the warm-up will be run. You should discuss these particulars with them at the last practice before a game. Here are guidelines for discussing these issues.

Pregame Meal

In general, the goal for the pregame meal is to fuel the player for the upcoming event, to maximize carbohydrate stores, and to provide energy to the brain. Some foods digest more quickly than others, such as carbohydrate and protein, so we suggest that players consume these rather than fat, which digests more slowly. Good carbohydrate foods include spaghetti, rice, and bran. Good protein foods include low-fat yogurt and boneless, skinless chicken. Players should eat foods that they are familiar with and that they can digest easily. Big meals should be eaten three to four hours before the game. Of course, players who don't have time for a big meal can use sport beverages and meal-replacement bars.

Clothing and Equipment

At the youth level, most teams wear same color T-shirts and shorts as the team uniform. Depending on the age group, where the game is played, and how far the team travels to the game, you should typically require that your players bring their uniforms and shoes with them to the game and change into them at the game site.

Some players may choose to wear eyewear, athletic braces, or mouth guards for protection and should be encouraged to do so.

Arrival Time

Your players need to adequately warm up before a game, so you should instruct them to arrive 30 to 45 minutes before game time (varying by age group) to go through the team warm-up (see next section). You can designate where you want the team to gather as they arrive. Consider making a team rule stating that players must show up 30 to 45 minutes before a game and go through the complete team warm-up, or they won't start.

Warm-Up

Players need to both physically and mentally prepare for a game once they arrive, and physical preparation involves warming up. We've suggested that players arrive 30 to 45 minutes before the game to warm up. You will want to conduct the pregame warm-up similar to practice warm-ups. Before game day, you should walk the players through the steps for how they will enter and where they will line up on the court for the warm-up. The warm-up should consist of a few brief games or drills that focus on skill practice, stretching, and exercises or activities that involve a range of motion, such as passing drills that get the players running while catching the ball.

You should refrain from delivering a long-winded pep talk, but you can help players mentally prepare for the game by reminding them of the skills they've been working on in recent practices and by focusing their attention on their strengths and what they've been doing well. Also take time to remind players that they should work as a team, play hard and smart, and have fun!

Coaching Tip

Although the site coordinator and officials have the formal responsibilities for facilities and equipment, you should know what to look for to ensure that the game is safe for all players (see "Facilities and Equipment Checklist" in appendix A on page 136). You should arrive at the game site 45 to 60 minutes before the game so you can check the facility, check in with the site coordinator and officials, and greet your players as they arrive to warm up.

Unplanned Events

Part of being prepared to coach is to expect the unexpected. What do you do if players are late? What if *you* have an emergency and can't make the game or will be late? What if the game is postponed? Being prepared to handle out-of-the-ordinary circumstances will help you if and when unplanned events happen.

If players are late, you may have to adjust your starting lineup. Although this may not be a major inconvenience, you should stress to your players that there are important reasons for being on time. First, part of being a member of a team is being committed to and responsible for the other members. When players don't show up, or show up late, they break that commitment. And second, players need to go through a warm-up to physically prepare for the game. Skipping the warm-up risks injury.

There may be a time when an emergency causes you to be late or miss a game. In these cases, you should notify your assistant coach, if you have one, or the league coordinator. If notified in advance, a parent of a player or another volunteer might be able to step in for the game.

Sometimes a game will be postponed because of inclement weather or for other reasons, such as unsafe court conditions. If the postponement takes place before game day, you must call every member of your team to let them know. If it happens while the teams are on-site and preparing for the game, you should gather your team members and explain why the game has been postponed. Make sure that all your players have a ride home before you leave—you should be the last to leave.

Communicating With Parents

The groundwork for your communication with parents will have been laid in the parent-orientation meeting, where the parents learned the best ways to support their kids'—and the whole team's—efforts on the court. You should encourage parents to judge success based not just on the outcome of the game, but also on how the kids are improving their performances.

If parents yell at the kids for mistakes made during the game, make disparaging remarks about the officials or opponents, or shout instructions on which tactics to use, you should ask them to refrain and to instead support team members through their comments and actions. These standards of conduct should all be covered in the preseason parent-orientation meeting.

When time permits, as parents gather before a game (and before the team has entered), you can let them know in a general sense what the team has been focusing on during the past week and what your goals are for the game. However, your players must come first during this time, so focus on your players during the pregame warm-up.

After a game, quickly come together as a coaching staff and decide what to say to the team. Then, if the opportunity arises, you can informally assess with parents how the team did based not on the outcome, but on meeting performance goals and playing to the best of their abilities. Help parents see the game as a process, not solely as a test that is pass or fail, or win or lose. Encourage parents to reinforce that concept at home.

For more information on communicating with parents, see page 15 in chapter 2.

During the Game

Throughout the game, you must keep the game in proper perspective and help your players do the same. You should observe how your players execute techniques and tactics and how well they play together. These observations will help you decide on appropriate practice plans for the following week. Let's take a more detailed look at your responsibilities during a game.

Tactical Decisions

Although you won't need to create a complex game strategy, as mentioned before, you will need to make tactical decisions in several areas throughout a game. You'll make decisions about who starts the game and when to enter

Keeping a Proper Perspective

Winning games is the short-term goal of your basketball program; helping your players learn the techniques and tactics and rules of basketball, how to become fit, and how to be good sports in basketball and in life is the long-term goal. Your young players are "winning" when they are becoming better human beings through their participation in basketball. Keep that perspective in mind when you coach. You have the privilege of setting the tone for how your team approaches the game. Keep winning and all aspects of the competition in proper perspective, and your young players will likely follow suit.

substitutes, about making slight adjustments to your team's tactics, and about dealing with players' performance errors.

Starting and Substituting Players

When considering playing time, make sure that everyone on the team gets to play at least half of each game. This should be your guiding principle as you consider starting and substitution patterns. We suggest you consider two options in substituting players:

1. *Substituting individually.*

   Replace one player with another. This offers you a lot of latitude in deciding who goes in when, and it gives you the greatest combination of players throughout the game. Keeping track of playing time can be difficult, but this task could be made easier by assigning it to an assistant or a parent.

   You may want to try substituting players by time left in the quarter, especially when working with younger age groups. For example, you can let a substitute know that she will play the last four minutes of each quarter, or that she will replace a player at the six-minute mark of the quarter. This will let the player know when she can expect to get into the game and will help the player be more prepared for her playing time.

2. *Substituting by quarters.*

   The advantage of substituting players after each quarter is that you can easily track playing time, and players know how long they will be in before they might be replaced. When substituting by quarters, you should still keep track of the actual number of minutes that each player is on the court.

Adjusting Team Tactics

At the 8 to 9 and 10 to 11 age levels, you probably won't adjust your team tactics, or plays, too significantly during a game. Rather, you'll focus on the basic tactics, and during breaks in the game, you'll emphasize the specific tactics your team needs to work on. However, coaches of 12- to 14-year-olds might have reason to make tactical adjustments to improve their team's chances of performing well and winning. As games progress, assess your opponents' style of play and tactics, and make adjustments that are appropriate—that is, those that your players are prepared for. You may want to consider the following examples when adjusting team tactics:

- How does your opponent usually initiate their attack? Do they aim to get around, over, or through your defense? This can help you make defensive adjustments.

- Who are the strongest players on the opposing team? The weakest players? As you identify strong players, you'll want to assign more skilled players to defend them.

- Are the opponent's forwards fast and powerful? Do they come to the ball, or do they try to run behind the defense and receive passes? Their mode of attack should influence how you instruct your players to defend them.

- On defense, does your opponent play a high-pressure game, or do they retreat once you've gained possession of the ball? Either type of defense could call for a different strategy from you.

- Ask your players, "What does the player you are guarding do well?" Then ask, "Do you think you can stop the player from doing that?" This will help players adjust their game to what the opponent does best.

Coaching Tip

Ask your players, "What does the player you are guarding do well?" Then ask, "Do you think you can stop the player from doing that?" This will help players adjust their game to what the oppnent does best.

Knowing the answers to such questions can help you formulate an effective game plan and make proper adjustments during a game. However, don't stress tactics too much during a game. Doing so can take the fun out of the game for the players. If you don't trust your memory, carry a pen and pad to note which team tactics and individual skills need attention at the next practice.

Correcting Players' Errors

In chapter 6, you learned about two types of errors: learning errors and performance errors. Learning errors are those that occur because players don't know how to perform a skill. Performance errors are made not because players don't know how to execute the skill, but because they make mistakes in carrying out what they do know.

Sometimes it's not easy to tell which type of error players are making. Knowing your players' capabilities helps you to determine if they know the skill and are simply making mistakes in executing it or if they don't know how to perform it. If they are making learning errors—that is, they don't know how to perform the skills—you should note this and cover it at the next practice. Game time is not the time to teach skills.

> **Coaching Tip**
> Designate an area on the sideline where players gather after coming off the court. In this area, you can speak to them either individually or as a group and make necessary adjustments.

If they are making performance errors, however, you can help players correct those errors during a game. Players who make performance errors often do so because they have a lapse in concentration or motivation, or they are simply demonstrating human error. Competition and contact can also adversely affect a young player's technique, and a word of encouragement about concentration may help. If you do correct a performance error during a game, do so in a quiet, controlled, and positive tone of voice during a break or when the player is on the sideline with you.

For those making performance errors, you must determine if the error is just an occasional error that anyone can make or if it is an expected error for a youngster at that stage of development. If the latter is the case, then the player may appreciate your not commenting on the mistake. The player knows it was a mistake and may already know how to correct it. On the other hand, perhaps an encouraging word and a "coaching cue" (such as "Remember to follow through on your shots") may be just what the player needs. Knowing the players and what to say is very much a part of the "art" of coaching.

Coach and Player Behavior

Another aspect of coaching on game day is managing behavior—both yours and your players'. As a coach, it is your responsibility to control emotions when aspects of the game, such as the plays you have designed or the defense you are playing, are not working as you or your players would have hoped.

Coach Conduct

You very much influence your players' behavior before, during, and after a game. If you're up, your players are more likely to be up. If you're anxious, they'll take notice, and the anxiety can become contagious. If you're negative, they'll respond with worry. If you're positive, they'll play with more enjoyment. If you're constantly yelling instructions or commenting on mistakes and errors, it will be difficult for players to concentrate. Instead, you should let players get into the flow of the game.

The focus should be on positive competition and on having fun. A coach who overorganizes everything and dominates a game from the sideline is definitely not making the game fun.

So how should you conduct yourself on the sideline? Here are a few pointers:

- Be calm, in control, and supportive of your players.
- Encourage players often, but instruct during play sparingly. Players should focus on their performance during a game, not on instructions shouted from the sideline.
- If you need to instruct a player, do so when you're both on the sideline, in an unobtrusive manner. Never yell at players for making a mistake. Instead, briefly demonstrate or remind them of the correct technique, and encourage them. Tell them how to correct the problem on the court.

You should also make certain that you have discussed sideline demeanor as a coaching staff, and that everyone is in agreement on the way the coaches should conduct themselves on the sideline. Remember, you're not playing for an Olympic gold medal! At this level, basketball competitions are designed to help players develop their skills and themselves—and to have fun. So coach in a manner at games that helps your players achieve these things.

Player Conduct

You're responsible for keeping your players under control. Do so by setting a good example and by disciplining when necessary. Set team rules for good behavior. If players attempt to cheat, fight, argue, badger, yell disparaging remarks, and the like, it is your responsibility to correct the misbehavior. Initially, this may mean removing players immediately from the game, letting them calm down, and then speaking to them quietly, explaining that their behavior is not acceptable for your team—and that if they want to play, they must not repeat the action. You must remember, too, that younger players are still learning how to deal with their emotions in addition to learning the game. As a coach, you must strive to remain calm during times when young players are having trouble controlling their emotions.

You should consider team rules in these areas of game conduct:

- Player language
- Player behavior
- Interactions with officials
- Discipline for misbehavior
- Dress code for competitions

Player Welfare

All players are not the same. Some attach their self-worth to winning and losing. This idea is fueled by coaches, parents, peers, and society, who place great emphasis on winning. Players become anxious when they're uncertain whether they can meet the expectations of others—especially when meeting a particular expectation is important to them also.

If your players look uptight and anxious during a game, you should find ways to reduce both the uncertainties about how their performance will be evaluated and the importance they are attaching to the game. Help players focus on realistic personal goals—goals that are reachable and measurable and that will help them improve their performance, all while having fun as they play. Another way to reduce anxiety on game day is to stay away from emotional pregame pep talks. Instead, remind players of the techniques and tactics they will use, and remind them to play hard, to do their best, and to have fun.

When coaching during games, remember that the most important outcome from playing basketball is to build or enhance players' sense of self-worth. Strive to keep that firmly in mind, and work hard to promote this through every coaching decision.

Keeping the Game Safe

Chapter 4 is devoted to player safety, but it's worth noting here that safety during games can be affected by how officials call the rules. If officials aren't calling rules correctly and this risks injury to your players, you must intervene. Voice your concern in a respectful manner and in a way that places the emphasis where it should be—on the players' safety. One of the officials' main responsibilities is to provide for players' safety. Both you and the officials are working together to protect the players whenever possible. Don't hesitate to address an issue of safety with an official when the need arises.

Opponents and Officials

You must respect the opponents and officials you encounter in your competitions. Without them, there wouldn't be a competition. Opponents provide opportunities for your team to test itself, improve, and excel. Officials help provide a fair and safe experience for players and, as appropriate, help them learn the rules of the game.

You and your team should show respect for opponents and officials by giving your best efforts and being civil. Don't allow your players to "trash talk" or taunt an opponent or an official. Such behavior is disrespectful to the spirit of the competition, and you should immediately remove a player from a game (as discussed previously in "Player Conduct") if that player disobeys your team rules in this area.

Remember, too, that officials at this level are quite often teenagers—in many cases not much older than the players themselves—and the level of officiating should be commensurate to the level of play. In other words, don't expect perfection from officials any more than you do from your own players. Especially at younger levels, they won't make every call, because to do so would stop the game every 10 seconds. You may find that officials at younger levels only call the most flagrant violations, those directly affecting the outcome of the game. As long as the calls are being made consistently on both sides and the violations are being addressed, most of your officiating concerns will be alleviated.

After the Game

When the game is over, join your team in congratulating the coaches and players of the opposing team, then be sure to thank the officials. Remember to check on any injuries players sustained during the game, and inform players on how to care for them at home. Be prepared to speak with the officials about any problems that occurred during the game. Then, hold a brief postgame meeting (as described in "Postgame Team Meeting") to ensure that your players are on an even keel, whether they won or lost.

Reactions Following a Game

Your first concern after a game should be your players' attitudes and mental well-being. You don't want them to be too high after a win or too low after a loss. This is the time you can be most influential in keeping the outcome in perspective and keeping them on an even keel.

When celebrating a victory, make sure your team does so in a way that doesn't show disrespect for the opponents. It's okay and appropriate to be happy and celebrate a win, but don't allow your players to taunt the opponents or boast about their victory. If your team was defeated, your players will naturally be disappointed. But, if your team has made a winning effort, let them know this. After a loss, help them keep their chins up and maintain a positive attitude that will carry over into the next practice and game. Winning and losing are a part of life, not just a part of sport. If players can handle both equally well, they'll be successful in whatever they do.

Postgame Team Meeting

Following the game, gather your team in a designated area for a short postgame meeting. Before this meeting, decide as a coaching staff what you will say and who will say it. Be sure that the staff speaks with one voice following the game.

If your players have performed well in a game, you should be sure to compliment them and congratulate them. Tell them specifically what they did well, whether they won or lost. This will reinforce their desire to repeat their good performances. Don't use this time after a game to criticize individual players for poor performances in front of teammates or attempt to go over tactical problems and adjustments. You should help players improve their skills, but do so at the next practice. Immediately after a game, players won't absorb much tactical information.

Finally, make sure your players have transportation home. Be the last one to leave to ensure full supervision of your players.

Developing Season and Practice Plans

We hope you've learned a lot from this book: what your responsibilities are as a coach, how to communicate well and provide for safety, how to teach and shape skills, and how to coach on game days. But game days make up only a portion of your season—you and your players will spend more time in practices than in competition. How well you conduct practice sessions and prepare your players for competition will greatly affect not only your players' enjoyment and success throughout the season, but also your own.

Fun Learning Environment

Regardless of where you are in your season, you must create an environment that welcomes learning and promotes teamwork. Following are seven tips that will help you and your coaching staff get the most out of your practices:

1. Stick to the practice times agreed on as a staff.

2. Start and end each practice as a team.

3. Keep the practice routine as consistent as possible so that the players can feel comfortable.

4. Be organized in your approach by moving quickly from one drill to another and from one period to another.

5. Tell your players what the practice will include before the practice starts.

6. Allow the players to take water breaks whenever possible.

7. Focus on providing positive feedback.

You may also want to consider using games to make practices more fun. In appendix B, you will find 17 gamelike drills. During your season, it may be fun to use the games toward the end of the week to add variety to your practices.

Season Plans

Your season plan acts as a snapshot of the entire season. Before the first practice with your players, you must sit down as a coaching staff and develop a season plan. To do this, simply write down each practice and game date on a calendar, and then go back and number your practices. These practice numbers will become the foundation of your season plan. Now you can work through the season plan, moving from practice to practice, to create a quick overview of what you hope to cover in each practice. You should note the purpose of the practice, the skills you will cover, and the activities you will use for that particular practice.

Following is more detailed information about season plans for each particular age group—ages 6 to 8, ages 9 to 11, and ages 12 to 14.

Season Plan for Ages 6 to 8

The players in this age group will be new to playing basketball, and you will be required to thoroughly explain and demonstrate basketball terms to your players. The ball-to-player ratio is 1:1, so plan for individual activities in your practices. You must also plan to take time to review skills learned in previous practices. For the 6- to 8-year age group, the following concepts and skills should be covered during the season:

> **Coaching Tip**
> While developing your season plan, keep in mind that you will want to incorporate the games approach into your practices. The games approach is superior to the traditional approach because it focuses on replicating the game environment. Using gamelike activities better develops the players both physically and mentally to the demands of the game.

- *Psychology:* Sharing, fair play, parental involvement, "how to play," emotional management
- *Fitness:* Balance, running, jumping, warm-up (introduce the idea of how to warm up), movement education
- *Technical skills:* Moving with and without the ball, footwork, dribbling, shooting, passing
- *Tactical skills:* Which basket to shoot at

Season Plan for Ages 9 to 11

Most of the players in this age group have had exposure to basketball, but some may still be newer to the sport. The season plan for this age group builds on the season plan for ages 6 to 8 as players refine fundamental skills. The ball-to-player ratio is 1:5, so as a coach you can plan for individual, pairs, and both small- and larger-group activities. For the 9- to 11-year age group, the following concepts and skills should be covered during the season:

- *Psychology:* Teamwork, confidence, desire, mental rehearsal, intrinsic motivation, handling distress, how to learn from each game, good sporting behavior, parental involvement, emotional management
- *Fitness:* Speed, strength, aerobic exercise
- *Technical skills:* Passing (chest, bounce, overhead, and one-handed push passes), dribbling (speed, control, crossover, and backup dribbles), shooting (layups, set and jump shots, and free throws), offensive and defensive footwork (slides, pivots, jump stops, and cuts)
- *Tactical skills:* Playing on and off the ball, passing around defensive players, fast break (2 on 1, 3 on 2, 4 on 3 drills; filling lanes; and outletting

the ball), communication, halftime analysis, offensive sets and specific plays, defensive principles including man-to-man and zone defense

Season Plan for Ages 12 to 14

At this stage, players are refining the skills they have learned from past years. This season plan builds on the plans for previous age groups and adds a few new skills. Many of the skills are the same as those presented in younger age groups, but in the 12- to 14-year age group, emphasis will be placed on different aspects of the game. For the 12- to 14-year age group, the following concepts and skills should be covered during the season:

- *Psychology:* Teamwork, confidence, desire, mental rehearsal, intrinsic motivation, handling distress, how to learn from each game, good sporting behavior, parental involvement, emotional management
- *Fitness:* Speed, strength, aerobic exercise
- *Technical skills:* Passing (overhead passes and passing off the dribble), shooting (set shots, power shots, and jump shots off the pass and dribble), post moves, defensive slides
- *Tactical skills:* Set plays for man-to-man and zone offenses, full-court defense for man-to-man and zone, fast break (lanes and secondary break), full-court press break on offense, inbounds plays, passing around the defense, jump ball situations

Practice Plans

Coaches rarely believe they have enough time to practice everything they want to cover. To help organize your thoughts and help you stay on track toward your practice objectives, you should create practice plans. These plans help you better visualize and prepare so that you can run your practices effectively.

First and foremost, your practice plans should be age appropriate for the age group you are coaching. The plans should incorporate all of the skills and concepts presented in the particular age group's season plan and should include activities that move from simple to more complex.

The practice plans for ages 6 to 8 should focus mostly on individual skill development. Games (such as those where players play 2v2 and 3v3) should be incorporated to help develop these skills.

The practice plans for ages 9 to 11 will be more advanced while still focusing on individual skill development. The advanced skills introduced at this level will focus on the basics of team offense and defense, as well as on team skills such as fast break transition and coordinated screens and cuts on offense.

The practice plans for the 12- to 14-year age group will begin to shift focus from individual skill development to further developing team offenses and defenses. This age group should focus on the skills that the players will need for their positions, such as post and perimeter play. The advanced skills introduced at this level will focus on additional aspects of team offense and defense, the fast break, and out-of-bounds plays.

Sample Practice Plan for Ages 6 to 8

Objective
To expose players to the basic skills of dribbling, passing, shooting, and rebounding

Equipment
One basketball per player

Activity	Description	Coaching points
Warm-up (3 minutes)	Players position on the baseline in groups of three or four and run line drills, focusing on pivots, runs, jump stops, and cuts.	• Balance • Agility • Coordination • Developing skills without the ball
Ball skills (10 minutes)	Each player has a ball. They each dribble to the coach and hand the ball to the coach. The coach tosses the ball away, and the players retrieve their ball and dribble it back to the coach. The coach can designate a different dribbling challenge to the players when the ball is tossed.	• Listening skills • Problem solving • Dynamic dribbling
Shadow dribble (5 minutes)	Each player dribbles a ball and follows the coach, who is also dribbling a ball. The coach executes basic dribbling moves and silly movements for players to mimic. The coach should include dribbling basics, such as crossover dribbles, and different movements while dribbling the ball.	• Dribbling and movement enhancement • Decision making
Knee tag (5 minutes)	Players position in a 10 × 15 yard area. Each player has a ball. Players dribble their ball and try to tag others on the knee while keeping the dribble alive. Each player is awarded one point for a tag.	• Physical fitness components • Dribbling and shielding skills • Looking around (vision)
2v2 game (15 minutes)	Players play a 2v2 game with very few rules in order to let them play and get the idea of movement with and without the ball.	• Summation of all challenges for the players • Stay out of their way and let them PLAY!
Cool-down (5 minutes)	*Body shapes:* Players create as many different shapes as they can with their body. The coach prompts change of movement.	• Lower heart rate and body temperature • Body control • Creativity and fun

Sample Practice Plan for Ages 9 to 11

Objective

To advance the basic skills of dribbling, passing, defense, shooting, and rebounding with a focus on the team concept

Equipment

One basketball per player

Activity	Description	Coaching points
Warm-up (10-15 minutes)	Players position in four groups on the baseline and run line drills, focusing on running forward and backward, starts and stops, and change of direction.	• Balance • Agility • Coordination • Improvement in athletic ability
Individual skill development (20-30 minutes)	Players position in three groups for drills that focus on dribbling, passing, and shooting skills. Players practicing dribbling focus on the crossover with a change of direction; players working on passing focus on passing around a defender and the overhead pass; players practicing shooting focus on form while shooting with a partner.	• Using either hand • Moving in either direction • Improving speed and agility
Team offense (15-20 minutes)	Players play 3v3 using the pick-and-roll to score, or they play 4v4 using the pick-and-roll and the screen away to get a teammate open for a shot. Points are awarded for each basket.	• Developing team offense • Establishing a gamelike structure for the offense • Using predetermined maneuvers before shots are taken
Team defense (15-20 minutes)	Players play 3v3 with defenders jumping to the ball on each pass. Points are awarded to the defense if the offense does not score. Play to 3 or 5 points.	• Developing team defense • Establishing a game-like structure for the defense • Communication on defense • Movement with the pass
Offense and defense (15-20 minutes)	Players practice 2-on-1 fast breaks. Introduce the concept of using the 3-on-2 fast break for attacking the defense on a break situation.	• Attacking in numbers-up situations • Communication
Cool-down (5-10 minutes)	Players perform full-court layup drills.	• Lower heart rate and body temperature • Developing gamelike skills

Sample Practice Plan for Ages 12 to 14

Objective

To further develop team offenses and defenses while advancing the basic skills needed to play in a game

Equipment

One basketball per player

Activity	Description	Coaching points
Warm-up (10-15 minutes)	Players position in four groups on the baseline and run line drills, focusing on running forward and backward, defensive slides, jumps, cuts, and jump stops.	• Balance • Agility • Coordination • Improvement in athletic ability
Individual skill development (20-30 minutes)	Players position in three groups for drills that focus on dribbling, passing, and shooting skills. Players practicing dribbling focus on the crossover dribble while adding the backup dribble; players practicing passing focus on passing on the move using chest or bounce passes; players practicing shooting focus on gamelike shooting situations, such as shooting by position or in numbers-up situations.	• Using either hand • Moving in either direction • Improving speed and agility
Team offense (15-20 minutes)	Players play 4v4 with rules such as squaring up with each pass and moving after each pass; or they play 5v5 using out-of-bounds plays and adding rules such as screening away for a teammate or using the pick-and-roll.	• Developing team offense • Establishing a gamelike structure for the offense
Team defense (15-20 minutes)	Players play 4v4 with defenders making adjustments for each pass, emphasizing the help side and ball side of the court; they advance to 5v5 that includes defending the screen away and the pick-and-roll. Award one point to the defense for an effective stop.	• Developing team defense • Establishing a gamelike structure for the defense • Defending the ball side and help side of the court • Defending cutters • Emphasis on zone defense
Offense and defense (10-15 minutes)	Players play 3v2 with a defensive trailer; or they play 5v5 with a baseline touch. Keep score by team and emphasize the fast break on offense.	• Scoring on the fast break and running the floor • Defensive and offensive transition
Cool-down (5 minutes)	Players perform shooting drills that focus on dribbling for the shot.	• Lower heart rate and body temperature • Developing gamelike skills

Appendix A

Related Checklists and Forms

This appendix contains checklists and forms that will be useful in your basketball program. All checklists and forms mentioned in the text can be found here. You may reproduce and use these checklists and forms as needed for your basketball program.

Facilities and Equipment Checklist

- ☐ The stairs and corridors leading to the gym are well lit.
- ☐ The stairs and corridors are free of obstruction.
- ☐ The stairs and corridors are in good repair.
- ☐ Exits are well marked and illuminated.
- ☐ Exits are free of obstruction.
- ☐ Uprights and other projections are padded, including the basket standards or poles.
- ☐ Walls are free of projections.
- ☐ Windows are located high on the walls.
- ☐ Wall plugs and light switches are insulated and protected.
- ☐ Lights are shielded.
- ☐ Lighting is sufficient to illuminate the playing area well.
- ☐ The heating and cooling system for the gym is working properly and is monitored regularly.
- ☐ Ducts, radiators, pipes, and so on are shielded or designed to withstand high impact.
- ☐ Tamper-free thermostats are housed in impact-resistant covers.
- ☐ If there is an overhanging track, be sure it has secure railings with a minimum height of three feet, six inches.
- ☐ The track has direction signs posted.
- ☐ The track is free of obstructions.
- ☐ Rules for the track are posted.
- ☐ Projections on the track are padded or illuminated.
- ☐ Gym equipment is inspected before and during each use.
- ☐ The gym is adequately supervised.
- ☐ Galleries and viewing areas have been designed to protect small children by blocking their access to the playing area.
- ☐ The gym (floor, roof, walls, light fixtures, and so on) is inspected on an annual basis for safety and structural deficiencies.
- ☐ Fire alarms are in good working order.
- ☐ Fire extinguishers are up to date, with note of last inspection.
- ☐ Directions are posted for evacuating the gym in case of fire.

From *Coaching Youth Basketball*, fourth edition, by ASEP, 2007, Champaign, IL: ASEP.

Informed Consent Form

I hereby give my permission for _____ to participate in _____ during the athletic season beginning on _____.
Further, I authorize the school to provide emergency treatment of any injury or illness my child may experience if qualified medical personnel consider treatment necessary and perform the treatment. This authorization is granted only if I cannot be reached and reasonable effort has been made to do so.

Parent or guardian: _____

Address: _____ **Phone:** ( ) _____

Cell phone: ( ) _____ **Pager number:** ( ) _____

Other person to contact in case of emergency: _____

Relationship to person: _____ **Phone:** ( ) _____

Family physician: _____ **Phone:** ( ) _____

Medical conditions (e.g., allergies, chronic illness): _____
_____
_____
_____
_____

My child and I are aware that participating in _____ is a potentially hazardous activity. We assume all risks associated with participation in this sport, including but not limited to falls, contact with other participants, the effects of the weather or traffic, and other reasonable-risk conditions associated with the sport. All such risks to my child are known and appreciated by my child and me.

We understand this informed consent form and agree to its conditions.

Child's signature: _____

Date: _____

Parent's or guardian's signature: _____

Date: _____

From *Coaching Youth Basketball*, fourth edition, by ASEP, 2007, Champaign, IL: ASEP. Reprinted, by permission, from M. Flegel, 2004, *Sport first aid*, 3rd ed. (Champaign, IL: Human Kinetics), 15.

Injury Report Form

Date of injury: _____ Time: _____ a.m./p.m.

Location: _____

Player's name: _____

Age: _____ Date of birth: _____

Type of injury: _____

Anatomical area involved: _____

Cause of injury: _____

Extent of injury: _____

Person administering first aid (name): _____

First aid administered: _____

Other treatment administered: _____

Referral action: _____

_____

_____

Signature of person administering first aid: _____

Date: _____

From *Coaching Youth Basketball*, fourth edition, by ASEP, 2007, Champaign, IL: ASEP.

Emergency Information Card

Player's name: _____ Sport: _____

Age: _____

Address: _____

Phone: _____

Provide information for parent or guardian and one additional contact in case of emergency.

Parent's or guardian's name: _____

Address: _____

Phone: _____ Other phone: _____

Additional contact's name: _____

Relationship to player: _____

Address: _____

Phone: _____ Other phone: _____

Insurance Information

Name of insurance company: _____

Policy name and number: _____

Medical Information

Physician's name: _____

Phone: _____

Is your child allergic to any drugs?   YES   NO

If so, what? _____

Does your child have other allergies (e.g., bee stings, dust)? _____

_____

Does your child have any of the following?   *asthma   diabetes   epilepsy*

Is your child currently taking medication?   YES   NO

If so, what? _____

Does your child wear contact lenses?   YES   NO

Is there additional information we should know about your child's health or physical condition?   YES   NO

If yes, please explain: _____

_____

_____

Parent's or guardian's signature: _____

Date: _____

From *Coaching Youth Basketball*, fourth edition, by ASEP, 2007, Champaign, IL: ASEP.

Emergency Response Card

Be prepared to give the following information to an EMS dispatcher.
(*Note:* Do not hang up first. Let the EMS dispatcher hang up first.)

Caller's name: _____

Telephone number from which the call is being made:_____

Reason for call: _____

How many people are injured: _____

Condition of victim(s): _____

First aid being given:_____

Location: _____

Address: _____

City:_____

Directions (e.g., cross streets, landmarks, entrance access):

From *Coaching Youth Basketball*, fourth edition, by ASEP, 2007, Champaign, IL: ASEP.

Appendix B

17 Gamelike Drills

In this appendix, you will find 17 gamelike drills that may be used in your basketball program. As a youth basketball coach, you can use gamelike drills during practices to help keep motivation and interest high and to keep the sport fun.

Two-Steppin'

Goal

To use pivots, drop steps, and jab steps to get free for shots.

Description

Play 3v3 in either the full or half court depending on the age group. When a player on the wing receives a pass, the player either (1) dribbles to the defender, stops, pivots, and shoots or (2) uses a jab or drop step, then dribbles around a defender for a layup. Two points are awarded if the player performs the pivot, jab, or drop step correctly and gets a shot off; an additional point is given for a made basket. One point is awarded for any made basket, whether made off of a pivot or jab or drop step. Play to three points for the 6 to 8 age group, five points for the 9 to 11 age group, and seven points for the 12 to 14 age group.

Variations

- To make the game easier, use a chair or other object in place of the defender so that the offensive player can get accustomed to the moves.
- To make the game more difficult, award the two "performance" points only on made baskets, or don't award any points for baskets not made off of a pivot or jab or drop step.

Drive-Through

Goal

To develop the ability to dribble under pressure.

Description

Play 3v3 or 4v4 in either the full or half court depending on the age group. Emphasize proper fundamentals, but place emphasis on dribbling under pressure by awarding the offense two points for scores off drives, one point if the offensive player can dribble the ball to the middle of the lane for a shot, and one point for all other baskets.

Variations

- To make the game easier, limit the number of dribbles that can be made by one player.
- To make the game more difficult, add another defensive player.

In My Dust

Goal

To use power dribbles and crossover dribbles to attack the basket.

Description

Play 3v3 or 4v4 in either the full or half court depending on the age group. Emphasize proper fundamentals, but place a special emphasis on effective dribbling by awarding one point each for made baskets, power dribbles, and crossover dribbles. Players should use these types of dribbles only as appropriate within the game situation. Points should not be awarded for ineffective or inappropriate use.

Variations

- To make the game more challenging, award points for only one specified move. For example, to focus on the crossover dribble, award one point to players for proper use of the crossover dribble, but require that they pass or shoot before they can be awarded another point. Defensive points may be awarded for steals, stopping the crossover, and so forth.

Passing Contest

Goal

To set up good shots through passing.

Description

Play 3v2 or 4v3 in either the full or half court depending on the age group. To place the emphasis on setting up good shots, award the offense one point for each successful pass and one point for each basket.

Variations

- To make the game easier, play 3v1 or 4v2.
- To make the game more difficult, do any of the following: play 3v3 or 3v4; award two points for a particular pass of your choosing; require that players use only a certain type of pass (i.e., chest, bounce, or overhead); or allow no dribbling.

Bucketmania

Goal

To score as many baskets as possible, using proper technique.

Description

Play 3v2 in the half court. Give the three offensive players five minutes to score as many baskets as possible against the two defensive players. After each made basket, a defensive player will rebound the ball and return it to the offense. After five minutes, switch the offense and defense, keeping one of the offensive players on offense so that play remains 3v2. The new offense will have five minutes to score as many baskets as possible.

Variations

- To make the game easier, play 3v1 or 4v2.
- To make the game more difficult, do any of the following: play 3v3 or 4v4; award two points for a particular type of shot of your choosing; or require that players only take a certain type of shot (e.g., jump shot, layup, shot off a dribble).

Room to Move

Goal

To create passing lanes and move to open space for better ball movement.

Description

Play 3v2 in the half or full court depending on the age group. The offense has the ball, and players pass and then move to a place on the court—point, wing, baseline, low post—that is adjacent to the ball. This emphasizes spacing by allowing the players to get to an open spot so one defender cannot guard two offensive players. Players can dribble, but the emphasis should be on little dribbling and crisp passing. Offensive players must make 10 passes; after the 10th pass, they can shoot and continue to shoot until they score or the defense rebounds.

Award one point for each pass successfully received and one point for a basket. Once a basket is made or the defense rebounds, begin again, this time with the two defenders moving to offense.

Variations

- To make the game easier, play 3v1.
- To make the game more difficult, play 3v3 or allow no dribbling.

Screen Door

Goal

To set effective screens to free up teammates.

Description

Play 3v2 in either the full or half court depending on the age group. The offense starts with the ball and must complete three passes before attempting a screen. The player with the ball should be positioned out on top (top of the key or circle above the three-point line); one teammate sets a screen for the other teammate, who cuts around the screen and looks for a pass from the player with the ball. The player with the ball can call out, "PR" (which signals to set a pick on the right side) or "PL" (which signals to set a pick on the left side), or the teammates can move on their own without the call.

The offense has five turns and is awarded two points for each successful screen and one point for each basket scored directly off the screen. (A screen is successful if it frees the teammate from her defender.) Reset the play after a shot is taken, whether the ball goes in or not.

Variations

- To make the game easier, play 3v1.
- To make the game more difficult, play 3v3.

Return to Sender

Goal

To score off of the give-and-go play.

Description

Play 3v3 in the half or full court depending on the age group. When offensive players have the ball, they look for an open teammate and make a pass. After a pass, the player cuts to the basket, looking for the return pass and the shot. Shots must be taken within five feet of the basket. Baskets scored directly off the give-and-go count for two points; other baskets count one point. Reset the offense after each play. The offense has five turns, then offense and defense are switched.

Variations

- To make the game easier, play 3v2.
- To make the game more difficult, award one point for offensive rebounds, which emphasizes blocking out by the defenders.

On the Line

Goal

To make free throws in game-winning situations.

Description

Players divide into two even teams and line up on each sideline on one half of the court. The first player in team A's line shoots two free throws, then the first player in team B's line shoots two free throws. Continue in this fashion, alternating between team A and team B, until all players have shot. The team with the most total points is the winner. If the game is tied after all players from both teams have shot, keep the same order of players and have a "sudden-death" shoot-off—with the first player from team A shooting one free throw, followed by the first player from team B shooting one free throw. The first time the tie is broken after both teams have shot, the game is over.

Variations

- To make the game easier, move the free throw line up one to three feet.
- To make the game more difficult, require the winning team to make at least four consecutive free throws in addition to making more free throws than its opponent.

Pickin' for Points

Goal

To score off of the pick-and-roll.

Description

Play 3v2 in the half or full court depending on the age group. The offense must complete three passes before attempting a pick-and-roll. The player with the ball positions out on top (top of the key or circle above the three-point line), while one offensive player sets a screen for the other offensive player. The player who set the screen then rolls to the basket, hand up, to receive the return pass for the shot. Award the offense two points for each successful pick-and-roll that results in a made basket. Reset the play after a shot is taken, whether the ball goes in or not. Switch teams after five plays.

Variations

- To make the game easier, play 3v1.
- To make the game more difficult, play 3v3.

Cleaning the Glass

Goal

To rebound using proper technique.

Description

Play 2v2 in either the full or half court depending on the age group. Each play begins with the coach shooting at the basket, intentionally missing the shot. The two offensive players try to rebound and score, and the defensive players also try to rebound. If the offense makes a basket or the defense gets the ball, the play is over. Each basket or rebound is worth one point. Switch offense and defense after five plays.

Variations

- To make the game easier, award two points for an offensive rebound.
- To make the game more challenging, require the offensive players to immediately shoot the ball, without a dribble, when they get the rebound.

Life in the Fast Lane

Goal

To convert fast break opportunities into baskets.

Description

Play 2v4 using a full court specific to the age group. One of the two offensive players takes a shot, but purposely misses it, to begin the game. The defense rebounds and runs a fast break, making the outlet pass and filling the lanes. The defense (which just converted from offense) attempts to stop the fast break. Award two points for a well-executed break and one additional point for finishing it off with a basket. Switch teams and repeat at the other end of the court.

Variations

- To make the game easier, play 1v4 or 1v3.
- To make the game more difficult, play 3v4 or 4v4, or allow no dribbling.

Seconds to Go

Goal

To score off of an inbounds play.

Description

Play 5v3 in the half court. Five seconds are placed on the clock, and an inbounds play is run. Award the offense one point for each basket scored before five seconds elapse.

Variations

- To make the game easier, play 5v2.
- To make the game more difficult, play 5v4 or 5v5.

Helping Hands

Goal

To provide help for a teammate.

Description

Play 3v3. Tape off a 3-foot-by-3-foot area about 15 to 20 feet from the basket from any angle on the court. This area is the "freeze zone"—that is, when a defender enters that zone, the defender must freeze. Instruct the offense to dribble so that the player guarding the dribbler enters the freeze zone. When this happens, the dribbler should dribble toward the basket (the other offensive players should not be clustered around this freeze zone or in the dribbler's path), and the "frozen" defender should call, "Help!" The defender's teammates respond appropriately, trying to cut off the dribbler and defend against passes to the dribbler's teammates. If the defense successfully provides help, it gets one point.

Note: If help is not provided well, but the offense misses its shot, the defense does not get a point. Successful help means cutting off the dribbler and not allowing an easy scoring opportunity.

Variations

- To make the game easier, play 3v4 or make the freeze zone farther away from the basket.
- To make the game more challenging, eliminate the freeze zone.

Cutting Off

Goal

To defend against screens.

Description

Play 2v2, 3v3, or 4v4. The offense must use screens in setting up plays. If the defense defends well against a screen (that is, no advantage is gained), the defense is awarded one point. If the offense gains an advantage on the screen, the defense loses one point. If the offense scores directly off of the screen, the defense loses two points. A play ends after the screen is set (the offense can shoot directly off the screen). From that point, the play is reset and the offense begins again. After five plays, switch sides.

Variations

- To make the game easier, play 2v3 or 3v4, or allow defenders to call out, "Switch!" and then switch players on screens.
- To make the game more difficult, require defenders to fight through or slide behind screens—no switching.

No Passing Zone

Goal

To cut off passing lanes and intercept passes.

Description

Play 3v3. The defense tries to cut off the passing lanes and intercept the ball. Each player on offense can dribble no more than three times before passing. Offensive players move to open spaces to receive passes and then look to hit open teammates with passes. The offense controls the ball for one minute. Then the teams switch sides. Within each one-minute period, the defense returns the ball to the offense if the defense steals it. Each steal counts for one point. Give each team five one-minute periods on defense.

Variations

- To make the game easier, play 3v4 or don't use dribbling.
- To make the game more difficult, play 4v3.

Picking Pockets

Goal

To create turnovers by stealing the ball.

Description

Play 3v4 or 2v3 in either the full or half court depending on the age group. The offense must complete four passes before attempting to shoot. The defense must use their defensive positioning to force a turnover or steal. Award two points to the defense for each turnover. As an option, you may also award one point for any of the following: forcing a dribbler to a sideline, funneling a dribbler to the middle (assuming defensive teammates are in the middle to help out), or forcing a dribbler to use the weak hand. Switch offense and defense after five minutes of play.

Variations

- To make the game easier, play 3v5 or 2v4.
- To make the game more difficult, play 3v3 or 4v4.

About ASEP

The fourth edition of *Coaching Youth Basketball* was written by the American Sport Education Program (ASEP) in conjunction with USA Basketball's Don Showalter.

Showalter has been the head boys' basketball coach and activities director at Mid-Prairie High School in Wellman, Iowa, since 1984. He has coached USA Basketball junior and youth development teams and coached the West squad in the 1999 McDonald's All-American game. Showalter has directed basketball camps all over the world, including Switzerland, Italy, Belgium, England, and Scotland.

ASEP has been developing and delivering coaching education courses since 1981. As the nation's leading coaching education program, ASEP works with national, state, and local sport organizations to develop educational programs for coaches, officials, administrators, and parents. These programs incorporate ASEP's philosophy of "athletes first, winning second."